CU00663894

Book 1 in this series: **"Delaware Before the Railroads"**
Book 2 in this series: **"Delaware from Railways to Freeways"**

"Delaware from Freeways to E-Ways"
Published by Dave Tabler
www.davetabler.com

Printed in the United States of America

ISBN 979-8-9870006-6-3
Library of Congress Control Number: 2024909770
Cover Design: Onur Burç

Acknowledgments

Many organizations offered their support to the development of this book. Heartfelt thanks to (in alphabetical order) Bombay Hook National Wildlife Refuge, Bowers Beach Maritime Museum, Camden Friends Meetinghouse, Delaware Agricultural Museum and Village, Delaware Art Museum, Delaware Public Archives, Delaware Historical & Cultural Affairs, Delaware Historical Society, Delaware Society for the Preservation of Antiquities, Delaware State University/William C. Jason Library, Delaware Tourism Office, Delaware Women's Hall of Fame, DNREC Division of Fish and Wildlife, Duck Creek Historical Society, First State National Historical Park, Friends of Old Dover, Inc., Free Library of Philadelphia, Friends of Old Swedes, Friends of Zoar, Inc., Georgetown Historical Society, Greater Harrington Historical Society, Hagley Museum & Library, Regina Higgins, Historic Odessa Foundation Inc., Johnson Victrola Museum, Knowles Museum, Lewes Historical Society, Marvel Carriage Museum, Milford Historical Society, Milford Museum, National Park Service, Nemours Estate, New Bedford Whaling Museum, New Castle Historical Society, Old Courthouse - Georgetown Historical Society, Charmaine Pardee, Pencader Heritage Museum, Presbyterian Historical Society, Seaford Museum, Heather Straub, Smithsonian Institution, Smyrna Museum, St. Jones Center for Estuarine Studies, Dr. Kenneth A. Tabler, University of Delaware Archives, US Postal Museum, Winterthur Museum Garden & Library, Zwaanendael Museum.

Preface

Welcome to *Delaware: From Freeways to E-Ways*, a survey of the First State's multifaceted twentieth-century history. The title might seem like an odd juxtaposition; nonetheless, freeways and digital ways do have a purposeful connection to each other.

Early twentieth century, people aspired to travel at what was the era's epoch light speed. Thus, the book opens with T. Coleman du Pont's pioneering highway project. The freedom of the freeway epitomized this titan's engineering ambition.

"E-Ways," meanwhile, short for "digital ways," harks back to the late 1990s. During that time, companies started adding an "e-" prefix to capitalize on the emerging world of e-commerce. This was done in an effort to comport with the rapidity of our changing world—to convey a sense of being on the cutting edge of technology.

The book ends by acknowledging Delaware's input to the building of these manifold digital ways. The University of Delaware's groundbreaking efforts have contributed several building blocks to the Internet's physical infrastructure. The school has also played a role in the commercialization of what the 1990s nicknamed the "information superhighway."

Between the two bookends of freeways and e-ways, I offer up stories of heroism, resilience, and innovation that define the Delawarean spirit. *Delaware: From Freeways to e-Ways* paints a nuanced portrayal of Delaware's complex twentieth century identity, from war heroes like James Phillip Connor, to enduring communities like the Nanticoke Native Americans.

The far-reaching influence of the du Pont family is central to Delaware's unfolding story. Numerous sectors felt the impact of their combined legacy. Du Pont heir Edmund H. "Ted" Harvey, for example, spearheaded environmental conservationism. DuPont Company chemist Wallace Carothers invented nylon. Wilmington Trust Company, owned by the family, pioneered Delaware's role in attracting myriad companies seeking incorporation.

I hope you acquire two takeaways by the end of your reading. First, a clearer understanding of Delaware's twentieth-century contributions. Second, an appreciation for how localized customs and stories are woven into the broader tapestry of our national narrative.

Contents

1900-1925 Concrete Ambitions

1926-1950 War & Resilience

1951-1975 Corporate Legacies & Societal Shifts

1976-2000 Toward Digital Horizons

Custom & Folklore Sidebars

The reedbird has been viewed through three lenses across Delaware history. Initially prized as game, the bird was later deemed a pest, and finally recognized as a fragile species warranting legal protection. The story of *Dolichonyx oryzivorus* (also known as the bobolink or ricebird) highlights how widely perspectives on nature can vary.

The *Delaware Advertiser and Farmer's Journal* mentions as early as 1824 a "fine string of reed-birds" gracing the market stalls. Reedbirds were both available and a delicacy, their flesh extremely juicy and tender. "What a luscious broil, or palatable pie they make," expounded the *Middletown Register* of August 1868. The birds' popularity led to soaring prices in city restaurants, making reedbirds an eagerly awaited and devoured epicurean event.

Yet, by the turn of the century, a shift occurred. An October 1, 1900, column in the *News Journal* noted that in New York, the reedbird was falling out of favor. "The up-to-date girl has finished with the toothsome reedbird," sniffed *Portia's New York Letter*, "and asks now for a stuffed partridge." Reedbirds were old news, at least for the urban elite.

In contrast, Delawareans remained steadfast in their love for the "reedies." (cont. on pg. 77)

Public libraries were scarce in Delaware at the dawn of the twentieth century, particularly in farming towns. Twelve women with a vision, inspired by the saying "mighty oaks from little acorns grow," banded together in 1902 to form the Acorn Club of Seaford. Their determination culminated in the founding of the Seaford Free Public Library. The Acorn Club's early meetings took place in rented rooms, with the ladies donating chairs, books, cups, and saucers. Each charter member contributed an inaugural book to the library. A core of donors supplied 100 paper-bound volumes, launching the simple reading room. By year's end, they had expanded the collection to 285 volumes.

Members regularly donated books and operated a traveling library, alternating duties among themselves. They continued this practice until hiring a part-time librarian, Miss Elizabeth Prettyman, for $1 a week. These humble beginnings paved the way for the circle's expanding ambitions and steadily improving facilities. By January 1904, the ladies had upgraded their quarters to nearby Bridgeville's Cottingham Block. Enhancements included carpeting, a piano, and an antique desk. The group made space accessible to "the country people" and to "men friends" once a month, guided by Mrs. Madison Willin's leadership. The club also initiated free reading sessions for the public every Friday evening. The ladies commenced distributing magazines, books, and newspapers at Seaford's railroad station and by February 1908 they started producing plays and entertainments to raise funds. Members generated "nearly one hundred dollars last evening— February 18—from a play entitled 'The Old Maids' Club," according to the *Morning News*. (cont. on pg. 77)

More businesses are incorporated in Delaware than people reside in the state. The one-million-plus registered corporations include two-thirds of America's Fortune 500 companies.

The First State's emergence as the premier spot for incorporation is marked by three key factors. The Chancery Court plays a vital role in drawing companies to Delaware. In addition, Delaware's extensive body of corporate case law is reassuring to conglomerates. Finally, incorporators can depend upon sophisticated banking support from specialized entities, such as the Wilmington Trust.

This financial institution came to play a central role from the start. Like so many aspects of Delaware corporate history, the trail leads back to the du Pont family. Three relatives — Coleman, Pierre, and Alfred (pictured above, left to right) — stunned their complacent family at the turn of the twentieth century. The DuPont Company's outstanding success caught the eyes of potential corporate raiders. The trio, in response, quickly acquired control to allay any possibility of a hostile takeover. (cont. on pg. 78)

Smyrna Opera House

The Smyrna Opera House, constructed in 1878, played a remarkable role in the life of native residents. The center functioned for over a half-century both as an entertainment venue and vibrant Smyrna neighborhood hub.

Local arts patrons enjoyed the melodies of an in-house orchestra by 1888, while community activities continued to proliferate. In 1900, the auditorium hosted presidential aspirant William Jennings Bryan.

Smyrna women Wilhelmina Wells, Helen Lewis, and Bertha Price competed in a fashion design contest in that same year. The storied walls of the Smyrna Opera House lent a dramatic backdrop to the competition for the coveted Demorest Gold Medal.

The arena saw a wealth of theatrical productions, such as the Dover Singing Society's 1903 comic opera "Reuben Scraggs." Two years and hundreds of events later, the Lyric Glee Club put on a benefit for the Teacher's Institute. (cont. on pg. 78)

Delaware speech has long harbored rich traditional idioms. Plenty of the state's colloquialisms have evolved in parallel with general American usage. The term "gumshoe," for example, originally referred to rubber galoshes. The meaning shifted over time due to the footwear's sound-muffling qualities, coming to signify a surreptitious detective.

Many customary First State expressions highlight a keen sense of observation and a deep connection with nature. Vivid descriptions like "pert as a cricket," "tadpole" (for small children), and "happy as a June bug" reveal a popular fondness for natural imagery.

Conversely, local folkloric clichés just as eagerly embrace human foibles and frailties. One of the more colorful figures of speech for intoxication, "high as a Georgia pine," borrows from the Deep South to aptly describe a state of lofty inebriation.

Many of the area's rural maxims weave astute insights of human behavior with elements of the natural world. Adages such as "If the draught is not right in your stove, the heat ebbs and flows," encapsulate armchair psychology. "He's independent as a wood sawyer" reflects keen observation of human character. These garden-variety proverbs came to be rooted in everyday experiences. (cont. on pg. 79)

The American architectural landscape underwent a notable metamorphosis in 1885 with the completion of the Home Insurance Building in Chicago. The city's ten-story edifice established a paradigm for what was considered a skyscraper.

Wilmington soon witnessed the construction of two likewise memorable establishments, the Equitable and Ford Buildings. Completed in 1892 and 1900 respectively, these adjacent nine-story towers did not achieve the height of the Chicago landmark, and so never earned recognition as bona fide skyscrapers. Nevertheless, they loomed over Market Street's skyline.

Wilmington's skyline would be further modified with the 1908 addition of the DuPont Building. Rising to a height of 12 stories, the structure occupied the entire block of Market between 10th and 11th Streets.

The du Pont family designed the building's height to compete with the Windy City standard as Delaware's first 'official' skyscraper. The monolith, from a challenging stance directly across the street, engulfed in shadow the shorter Equitable and Ford Buildings.

The DuPont Building set an early benchmark, but the structure's height held only a short-time record. (cont. on pg. 79)

Birth of the Delaware Art Museum

The anticipation among Wilmington's circle of artists, collectors, and philanthropists mounted over several months. The November 1912 event initially aimed to celebrate the life's work of the recently deceased "father of illustration," Howard Pyle. Yet the exhibition sponsor, the Wilmington Society of Fine Arts, harbored a secondary ambition. They sought to amass, under a single roof, artworks by Pyle's first-ranked protégés. This distinctive assembly, for the first time, repatriated Delaware's finest art talent from private nationwide collections. An array of permanent loan selections subsequently spearheaded the Delaware Art Museum's establishment. (cont. on pg. 80)

T. Coleman du Pont was among the first turn-of-the-century Delawareans to anticipate the future of highway traffic. This corporate executive had repeatedly dealt with substandard roads during his approximately 100-mile trip between Wilmington and an estate in Cambridge, Maryland. "With the advent of the automobile," du Pont wrote in a letter to the State Highway Department, "I realized the wonderful development of which our little State is susceptible and that the first essential for this development is a well laid out system of highways traversing all sections of the State." He went on to point out the obvious —the backbone of such a system must be a main North and South highway, modeled after the great boulevards of Europe. And so, in February 1911, du Pont announced his willingness to advance Delaware $1,000,000 to construct just such a road. Du Pont's generosity spurred the General Assembly, which hastened to pass the groundbreaking Boulevard Corporation Act enabling a private corporation to build a public thoroughfare. According to the plan, once a section at least ten miles long was finished, that portion would be transferred to the state, free of charge. (cont. on pg. 80)

·FROM·THE·LAND·OF·HOLLY·

The holly tree, adopted as the state tree in 1939, holds an enduring place in Delaware's rich folklore.

Renowned author C.A. Weslager of Wilmington observed a poignant Nanticoke tradition of herb doctors and magic cures: mothers brewed a tea from boiled holly ashes for their children as a remedy for whooping cough.

The holly, besides being crucial to the early medicinal practices of Delaware's Native American communities, became a twentieth-century seasonal business of the Delmarva peninsula. A bustling cottage industry of wreath-making produced hand-crafted decorations, nurturing cultural pride during Christmas celebrations. (cont. on pg. 81)

Holly packing house in Milford

Right: *Frances (Sheridan) Haut, 10 years old in 1918, years later recalled New Castle's "Canary Cottage" near Witt's Bakery on Delaware St. This rooming house was named not for its color but for the yellowed tongues of the women working with tetryl in the plant (below).*

New Castle's Bethlehem Loading Plant, a subsidiary of Bethlehem Steel, assembled, packed, and shipped artillery ammunition during World War I. The complex, constructed rapidly to meet the sudden demand, played an indispensable role and operated continuously throughout the conflict. The Allies' appetite for munitions swelled as the war reached a climax in 1918. This demand prompted the facility to expand operations at an unprecedented pace.

Doughboys went off to fight, while women and older men were left to bear the home front responsibilities. They filled factories and offices, becoming the backbone of the domestic war effort. Rapid growth led to a surge in worker demand, but housing was scarce. The community's churches pitched in, offering shelter. "Preparations are nearing completion at the parish house for the housing of fifty girls who are to be employed at the Bethlehem Loading Company," the *News Journal* reported on August 13. "The parish house is the property of Immanuel Protestant Episcopal Church. It is through the rector and parishioners that this splendid building is offered to the girls." (cont. on pg. 82)

BYGUM! THEM SUFFRAGETTES BE GITTIN EVERY THING.

QUESTION.

HOW CAN THIS BE A 'GOVERNMENT OF THE PEOPLE AND BY THE 'PEOPLE' IF ONLY ½ OF THE PEOPLE VOTE!

SUFFRAGIST

ANTI-SUFFRAGIST.

The United States Congress passed the 19th Amendment to the Constitution in June 1919, granting women the right to vote. But the hardest part came next: the amendment's formal submission to the states for ratification. As 1919 gave way to 1920, momentum grew. The year opened with 22 states' approval. Kentucky and Rhode Island quickly followed. Oregon became the 25th state to ratify on January 13. Eleven states still needed to say "yes." (cont. on pg. 83)

Women depart Wilmington train station for a suffrage demonstration, May 2, 1914

Delaware's tradition of agricultural fairs dates back to 1763, when farmers and businessmen gathered in Dover to sell livestock and market merchandise. Throughout the 1800s, organizers staged similar events in Odessa, Wilmington, Laurel, Middletown, and Bridgeville. These fairs provided a platform to discover the latest technology and showcase their top-tier farm equipment and animals. Dover's Fairview Park in 1855 hosted the first of many expanded fairs and, despite facing pushback, garnered great success. "God forbid that its like should ever be seen again," complained a letter to the editor in the *Wilmington Daily Republican*. The writer vehemently criticized the fair management's lackadaisical attitude towards under-the-table gambling operations. Over minor objections, the annual Dover event flourished and eventually became the largest fair in the state. The gathering had assumed the title of the Delaware State Fair by 1896, marking the event's standing in the region. Fairview Park came alive for a full week from September 21-26, celebrating the occasion's forty-first anniversary. (cont. on pg. 84)

KENT & SUSSEX COUNTY FAIR ASSOCIATION, INC.
Harrington, Del.

Five Big Days

Five Big Nights

"FAIR COMRADES"

July 24, 25, 26, 27, 28, 1923

F. Scott Fitzgerald once declared, "There are no second acts in American lives," alluding to the idea that failures in business or love irreversibly define a person's path. Yet, Clarence Welch, a Milford businessman proved an exception to said rule at age of 50 . He rose from earlier mistakes that cost him a lifelong friendship, a good reputation, and almost his life.

The newfound public craving for ice cream on-the-go during the late 1800s created a demand for disposable spoons. The use of wooden spoons became a particularly popular choice in soda fountains and ice cream parlors. J. H. Mulholland Company emerged as a player in a new niche—gumwood ice cream spoons. The Milford/Philadelphia company started in 1922, quickly making a name for itself. *(Milford plant, 1922, below)*

Clarence Welch, a daring young Mulholland Company office boy, rose through the ranks with dedication and sharp business acumen. By 1942, he became treasurer and general manager, eventually becoming executive vice-president, vested with the company's day-to-day management in 1948. Driven by this new direction and his accompanying status as the largest individual stockholder, Welch steered Mulholland Company to national prominence. His ascent was remarkable, but unforeseen challenges awaited, ready to test both his personal and professional mettle. Clarence Welch's bond with company salesman Howard W. Black, forged at the onset of their careers at Mulholland, played a key role in his aspirations within the firm.

Black's occasional loans to Welch underscored their camaraderie built over years. Harboring ambitions to acquire the J.H. Mulholland Company, Welch crafted a clandestine plan. He envisioned borrowing a portion of the needed capital from Black, albeit without Black's questioning the purpose, while misappropriating the rest from the company's coffers. (cont. on pg. 84)

Raymond Watson Kirkbride's maiden voyage across the Atlantic in 1923 was more than mere overseas travel. The trip realized an educational vision that continues to reverberate in American academia. The World War I veteran was a faculty member at the University of Delaware. He established a limited program — the Delaware Foreign Study Plan — in France with a cohort of eight students *(below)*. Kirkbride's motivation stemmed from a deep-seated belief that global exposure could bolster peace and understanding. His time in France as part of the American Expeditionary Forces fundamentally altered the soldier's views on cross-cultural relations. For the future professor, international conflicts were a byproduct of ignorance and mistrust, which education could effectively remedy. He sought to translate his war experiences into an academic curriculum designed to shape future diplomats and world citizens. Upon his return to the United States, Kirkbride met with University of Delaware President Dr. Walter Hullihen, whose endorsement provided the idea with institutional validation. The proposed comprehensive curriculum covered various subjects—history, politics, literature, art—from the French cultural point of view. The syllabus also incorporated industrial site visits, meetings with French citizens, and social events aimed at enriching the students' understanding of the host nation. Kirkbride's unflagging enthusiasm and charismatic personality captivated both his students and colleagues. (cont. on pg. 85)

Whether prepared through grilling, stewing, frying, baking, or broiling, chicken has become an American dietary staple thanks to the extensive poultry sheds in Delmarva. These large operations play a crucial role in the nation's food chain, connecting our dinner tables with quality meat day after day in a new era of American consumerism.

Farmers of the early 20th century raised birds primarily for their eggs. Only when the chickens aged, and their egg-laying slowed, did they find their way into the stew pot. This paradigm witnessed a consequential metamorphosis, all thanks to the persistent efforts of one individual, Ocean View housewife Cecile Long Steele. A pioneer of her home state's broiler industry, this lady found her footing in the business quite serendipitously. Due to a clerical error at her supply hatchery, Cecile in 1923 received a shipment of 500 chicks, even though she only recalled ordering 50. This delivery sent her scrambling. (cont. on pg. 86)

1983.1 STEELE

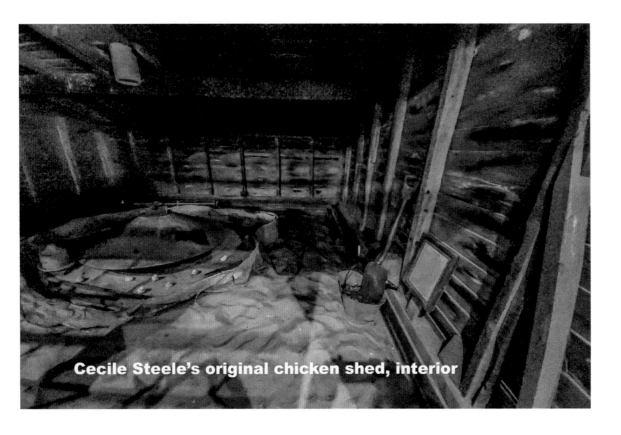

Cecile Steele's original chicken shed, interior

Baseball Hall of Famer

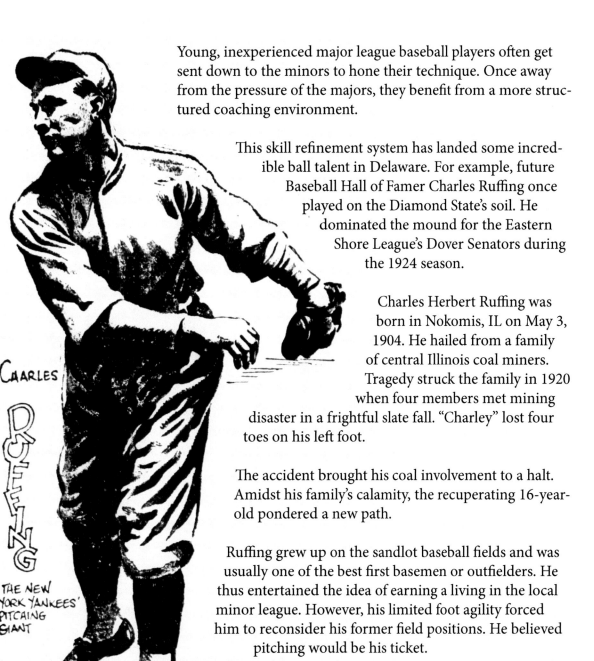

CHARLES RUFFING

THE NEW YORK YANKEES' PITCHING GIANT

Young, inexperienced major league baseball players often get sent down to the minors to hone their technique. Once away from the pressure of the majors, they benefit from a more structured coaching environment.

This skill refinement system has landed some incredible ball talent in Delaware. For example, future Baseball Hall of Famer Charles Ruffing once played on the Diamond State's soil. He dominated the mound for the Eastern Shore League's Dover Senators during the 1924 season.

Charles Herbert Ruffing was born in Nokomis, IL on May 3, 1904. He hailed from a family of central Illinois coal miners. Tragedy struck the family in 1920 when four members met mining disaster in a frightful slate fall. "Charley" lost four toes on his left foot.

The accident brought his coal involvement to a halt. Amidst his family's calamity, the recuperating 16-year-old pondered a new path.

Ruffing grew up on the sandlot baseball fields and was usually one of the best first basemen or outfielders. He thus entertained the idea of earning a living in the local minor league. However, his limited foot agility forced him to reconsider his former field positions. He believed pitching would be his ticket.

Doc Bennett of a nearby semi-professional league got young Ruffing into pitching with the minor league Danville Three-I club *[Illinois-Indiana-Iowa]*. Boston Red Sox scouts noticed the young pitcher's talent immediately. Boston Americans, the Sox owners, acquired the 19-year-old in August 1923 for $4,000. (cont. on pg. 86)

The Delaware State Police came into being during the Roaring Twenties. The flapper era also birthed the Department's immediate precursor: the Citizens' Highway Police Reserve Corps (CHPRC). This volunteer force turned out to be ill-equipped to rein in widespread disregard for the rules of the road. The botched experiment provides a vivid case study, illustrating the perils tied to an untrained, undisciplined brigade devoid of accountability. The State Highway Commission authorized the deployment of a citizens' highway police from 1921 to 1923. This initiative aimed to supplement the limited resources of the professional State Highway Police. The newcomers served for a three-month period and were empowered to enforce the same laws as the paid force. The appointees did not receive the same rigorous indoctrination and discipline as qualified law enforcement officers. (cont. on pg. 87)

Prohibition's onset caught the U.S. Coast Guard flat-footed in their new role of combating rum-running. The maritime service was insufficiently prepared to handle the daunting task of patrolling Delaware Bay's 782 square miles. The Coast Guard established 19 stations along the DE/MD coastlines, each manned by a team of six. Along the New Jersey coast, 41 stations were set up, each staffed by a mere trio of guardsmen. This deployment soon revealed itself as grossly inadequate for the looming challenges. Compounding the issue, the conclusion of the Great War saw Coast Guard funding severely stretched. The federal government, in a bid to curtail military expenditures, had slashed budgets across the board. The authorities found themselves grappling with a formidable mandate. (cont. on pg. 87)

Coast Guard approaches rum-runner ship off NJ coast 1928

Early 20th-century commercial sweet potato farming and marketing in southern Delaware is a tale of promise, growth, and sudden decline. The cash crop's rise begins with a 19th-century acknowledgment of wide market potential from those who savored the fall favorite. The versatile and delicious root vegetable, part of the morning glory family, became a staple with European settlers.

The prolific, easy growing "sweets," when harvested, have a bright pink skin and deep orange flesh. Vine propagation begins with bare-root nursery slips hand planted in raised beds of well-drained sandy loam soil.

"The sweet potatoes of Southern Delaware have a richness and sweetness of flavor, which we do not find in the Carolina potato nor even those grown on the rich fresh soils of Texas," beamed the 1868 *Delaware State Directory.*

Sussex County agribusiness harnessed the sweet potato as a primary cash crop at the turn of the 20th century. County production quadrupled after 1900, spanning more than 9,800 acres by then. Between 1900 and 1930, the peninsula's combined bushels exceeded all but two southern sweet potato-producing states. (cont. on pg. 88)

Dynamiting Indian River Bay Inlet 1928

Indian River Bay coastal waterway has always been a vital gateway to Sussex County's southern interior, even after the advent of the railroads. The bay's ocean connection hastened Delaware's European immigrants to develop the area early on. Revolutionary War General John Dagsworthy, for example, laid out the town of Dagsboro there in the late 18th century. Centered around his extensive plantation holdings, the settlement took shape under General Dagsworthy's design.

Indian River Bay Inlet's natural beauty has belied numerous challenges for sailors from time immemorial. The treacherous passage is shallow and a minefield of sand bars.

Rapid tidal action caused by the bay's ocean proximity perennially sweeps voluminous amounts of sand into the cove. European settlers had to use flat-bottomed boats with shallow drafts to navigate the narrow channels. (cont. on pg. 88)

Delaware's canning industry peaked during the Progressive Era, waning with the rise of frozen foods in the 1940s. From Seaford to Wilmington, families converged on farms and factories, engaging in the entire production line from seeding to shipping canned goods nationwide. By 1900, the state dominated in canning tomatoes, beans, peas, and sweet potatoes, employing a quarter of its labor force in this sector around 1910. Notable canning firms included H.P. Cannon & Son, of Bridgeville, and Richardson & Robbins Co., of Dover. Illustration Library of Congress

Oysters have profoundly influenced Delmarva in every aspect, from harvesting to consumption, for as long as people have been eating this ancient shellfish. One and all prized the Delaware Bay "white gold" for its unique taste and high-quality meat. An appetite for Eastern oysters grew with the nation's mid-19th century population. The transcontinental railroad's completion further fueled demand and provided access to eager markets.

The fully integrated industry truly took off following the Civil War. Starting in 1866, Delaware required a license to use harvesting tools such as tongs, scrapes, or dredges. Bay watermen that year harvested an impressive 10,000,000 bushels of oysters between September and April. They followed the longstanding tradition of fishing only during months with an "R" in their names.

The custom has a practical origin that blends culinary wisdom with an understanding of oyster biology and environmental considerations. These guidelines stem from pre-refrigeration and cleverly align with the natural cycles of oysters, and safety concerns. During the warmer months, from May through August, oysters are often in their spawning phase. (cont. on pg. 89)

"Panned, broiled, stewed, a la king or creamed, the oyster prepared by a lower Delaware gastronomic artist is sufficient to bring forth paeans of joy."

Wilmington
News Journal

Civilian Conservation Corps

President Franklin D. Roosevelt, recognizing the need to address the Great Depression's unprecedented unemployment and economic stagnation, proposed in 1933 the Civilian Conservation Corps (CCC). Driven by his vision for national recovery and innovative use of natural resources, Roosevelt outlined the program and pushed for legislative approval, coordinating with secretaries and advisors to ensure the bill's completion and submission to Congress.

Thanks to Roosevelt's strategic leadership and the broad support he garnered, the CCC legislation passed swiftly. This emergency measure, spearheaded by Roosevelt, led to the establishment of 2,650 CCC camps nationwide, employing over half a million individuals. The first camp, Camp Roosevelt, began operations on April 17, 1933, near Luray, VA. Delaware followed with camps in Lewes and Milford, with the final state camp erected in 1938 near Leipsic.

Each CCC camp blueprint mandated six large buildings with electric lights and indoor plumbing, including barracks, a medical unit, a mess hall, officers' quarters, a recreation room, and warehouses. Roosevelt's direct involvement and leadership were crucial in the CCC's establishment, which aimed to put thousands of unemployed young men to work on essential conservation projects, such as forest management, soil erosion, and flood control. (cont. on pg. 90)

"Mosquito Ditch Control CCC" by Jack Lewis 1936

The Great Depression swirled through the mid-1930s, bringing both personal and political unrest. The tempest blew right through the 1934 halls of Congress. President Franklin D. Roosevelt proposed the Social Security Act to alleviate these miseries. His legislation promised unemployment and disability insurance, plus old age provisions. The business community pushed back immediately, citing the burden of shared costs. They assembled an organized voice of dissent comprised of corporate leaders from the likes of General

"TENTING TONIGHT ON THE OLD CAMP GROUND."

Motors, Standard Oil, and U.S. Steel. Corporate leaders gathered in August 1934 at New York's Union League Club. (cont. on pg. 90) *Liberty league lawyers (below) discuss a report on the (un) constitutionality of the Wagner Labor Relations Act. From the left: R.E. Desvernine, Chairman of the Lawyers committee; Jouett Schouse and Earl F. Reed.*

Delaware began embracing rural electrification in May 1935. President Franklin Roosevelt appointed Morris L. Cooke as head of the Rural Electrification Administration (REA). Cooke was on a mission to light up the lives of receptive farmers. Electric infrastructure began to take shape locally, reaching across the state from pole to pole. The excitement of electrification was coming!

Cooke's industry stump speech emphasized the enormous profit this program promised for home product manufacturers and existing private utilities. "The opportunity is presented to industry," he said, "to develop substantial appliances of quality at low cost in view of the vast sales field which is now opening up for them." (cont. on pg. 91)

Above: *An unidentified farm woman happily poses for a* News Journal *photographer on May 13, 1938, demonstrating her delight at being able to forego the smoky old kerosene lamp and switch to overhead electric lights. photos above and opposite page upper right:* The News Journal – *USA TODAY NETWORK*

Hurricanes, while not an everyday Delaware occurrence, have etched their mark throughout the state's history. High winds, having gathered strength over Delaware Bay's open waters, lash the shoreline. (cont. on pg. 92)

generated by Dall-E

The year 1939 marks a notable period in Delaware art history, owing to the remarkable achievements under the Federal Art Project (FAP). This twelve-month period also represented the zenith of the agency's influence and success.

The Federal Art Project, under the umbrella of Roosevelt's Works Progress Administration, operated actively from 1935 to 1943.

The organization played a vital role in providing employment for artists during the Great Depression. The arts group sponsored a diverse array of creative endeavors, including murals, sculptures, and paintings. Three murals by Edward L. Grant, Walter Pyle, and Andrew Doragh found their way to the walls of Georgetown High School; Claymont High School displayed Walter Pyle's "History of Claymont" mural; Howard High School hung Edward Loper's newly created paintings; and Smyrna High School featured six murals, by Edward L. Grant, Walter Pyle, and Stafford Good, including the latter's "Cavalcade of Delaware." (cont. on pg. 92)

The Fenwick Island Lighthouse, once a beacon for seafarers, now stands as a silent sentinel to the community preservation of Delaware's rich maritime history. Lord Baltimore granted this piece of land in 1682 to an English farmer named Thomas Fenwick. The Delaware Bay shipping trade had prospered for two centuries by the mid-1800s. Lighthouses at Ocean City, MD, and Cape Henlopen had been in service for decades. But the era's lighthouse network

exhibited numerous shortcomings. Their navigational safety beams fell too short to warn of a dangerous shoal extending five miles out from Fenwick Island. Responding to pressure to improve lighthouse service, Congress established a 9-member Lighthouse Board in 1852. The board acted to commission the Fenwick Island Lighthouse in 1858, equipping it with the latest lighthouse technology. They positioned the signal just a few feet from the Trans-Peninsular Marker, which defines Delaware's southern border with Maryland. The 82-foot-high, white-washed brick tower first cast a beam on August 1, 1859. (cont. on pg. 93)

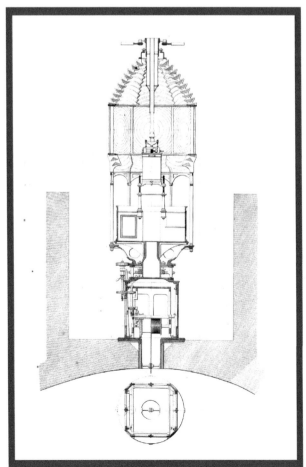

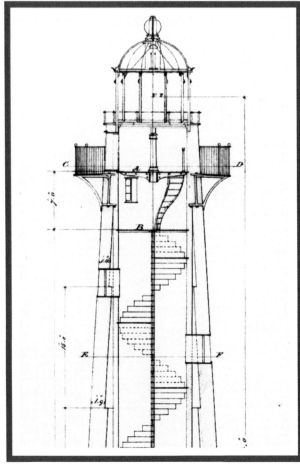

generated by Dall-E

The practice of eminent domain in the early twentieth century often left deep scars in American communities. Governmental entities could, at the stroke of a pen, forcibly acquire private land. This policy set the stage in New Castle County for a poignant 1941 drama. The Levy Court's decision to construct a new airport sent shockwaves through residents. Among them, the story of John T. Hopkins and his family stands out, vividly illustrating the deeply personal impact of these broad political decisions on individuals and their day-to-day lives. Meanwhile, a far more ominous shadow was being cast across the Atlantic. The global stage was set for a conflict that would soon demand unprecedented measures from nations far and wide, including the United States. Adolf Hitler's momentous European war campaign had consumed most of the continent, inciting real fear of an attack on America's East Coast. Delaware responded with plans to build the state's first public airstrip, known initially as Greater Wilmington Airport. (cont. on pg. 93)

The remnants of Fort Miles, situated amid shifting sand dunes in Delaware's Cape Henlopen State Park, tell a tale of wartime vigilance. The fort originally spanned 1,550 acres. Today, the World War II site preserves a vivid embodiment of America's coastal military architecture. The US Army established Fort Miles in 1940 as part of the "Harbor Defense." The fortification honors General Nelson A. Miles, who served in the Civil War, the Indian Wars, and the Spanish-American War. Fort Miles safeguarded

Delaware Bay, a vital regional maritime access point to the East Coast's industrial centers. Army command in 1941 stationed the 261st Coast Artillery at the fort. The garrison was assigned to defend Dupont's Wilmington complex, guard the city of Philadelphia, and shield oil refineries along the Delaware River in Pennsylvania and New Jersey. At the peak of its operation, Fort Miles functioned as a small town with 2,500 men and women, ranking among the largest seacoast fortifications in the United States. *Right:* German U-Boat Lt. Commander Thilo Bode. (cont. on pg. 94)

The Civilian Aviation Administration (CAA) in late 1940 made a strategic planning move, one prompted by the gathering storm clouds of World War II. The master plan underscored the necessity of quickly building a series of East Coast municipal airports, each one serving as a vital link in an Atlantic defense network. Atlantic seaboard state and local government participation was crucial. The CAA was prepared to underwrite the construction of a string of selected sites. After that, the states had the responsibility to manage the new facilities. The CAA proposed the construction of an airfield in each of Delaware's three counties. However, state officials balked over the provision of providing financial support. The offer was then passed down to the county governments, with New Castle and Sussex counties accepting the deal. Kent County declined and handed the opportunity to the city of Dover. After much deliberation, Dover leaders agreed and purchased 587 acres southeast of town to establish a new municipal airfield. The $35,000 gamble proved, in hindsight, to be not only forward-looking but also a wise investment for the city. (cont. on pg. 95)

Of the fourteen Delawareans awarded the Congressional Medal of Honor, only Sergeant William Lloyd Nelson *(right)*, a 25-year-old farm boy from Middletown, died in battle.

The World War II Army enlistee took command of an April 24, 1943, assault squad. Their mission: clear a path for the US Army's Sixtieth Infantry Regiment. Their target: the German-controlled city of Bizerte, set in the rugged landscape near Tunis, in Tunisia.

Nelson and the Sixtieth engaged in combat on a North African hill, Djebel Dardyss, that day. They converted this typically unremarkable location into a critical stronghold. This strategic move effectively halted a German attack.

The Army inducted Nelson at Fort Dix on January 9, 1941. He was among America's "first million" called to arms before the Pearl Harbor attack. The recruit tackled boot camp at Fort Bragg in North Carolina and advanced to the rank of corporal. His training intensified with the advent of Pearl Harbor's destruction. (cont. on pg. 96)

Born into a modest Wilmington family, James Phillip Connor *(below)* excelled at basketball and football at St. Mary's Parochial School. He left after the 8th grade to work for a local leather company. The US Army drafted Connor in January 1941. He completed basic training at Fort Bragg.

Connor deployed to North Africa in November 1942 with the 9th Infantry Division. By August 1944, Sgt. Connor had been reassigned to the 3rd Infantry. This set the stage for a life-changing role in "Operation Dragoon" on the French Riviera.

German soldiers controlled Cape Cavalaire on France's Mediterranean coast as of August 15. The Allies viewed the locale as a tactical linchpin. Capturing the cape would open access to a vital port for supplies and the potential for strategic troop advancement. (cont. on pg. 96)

Many unmarried Americans felt adrift amid the cultural upheaval of the early twentieth century. The suffragette movement, advocating for women's rights, surged forward, challenging traditional gender roles. Prohibition, which banned the sale of alcohol, reshaped interpersonal dynamics by altering socializing patterns. Furthermore, the rapid expansion of industrializing cities provided a new backdrop for relationships. (cont. on pg. 97)

generated by Dall-E

DuPont chemist Wallace Hume Carothers' invention of nylon in 1937 arrived as a boon for economically struggling Sussex County. Prior to DuPont's establishment of a new nylon production facility in the area, residents eked out a living primarily through farming and other local endeavors.

Carothers, born in the Midwest in 1896, from a young age burned with an insatiable curiosity about chemistry and machines. The University of Illinois awarded him a PhD in organic chemistry in 1924. He went on to teach the subject at Harvard. His research into the potential of combining chemicals with water to produce fibers caught the attention of DuPont executives.

Following World War I, DuPont sought corporate diversification and identified Carothers as a key player for new product development. They courted him to head the organic chemistry research unit, offering to double his salary and giving him unfettered exploratory freedom.

Carothers worried increased pressures of the corporate versus the academic world would exacerbate his struggles with crippling depression. But he accepted Dupont's package and joined them in the winter of 1928. (cont. on pg. 98)

Wilmingtonian Pauline A. Young rose to become a luminary in the fields of education, civil rights, and library science. Born in 1900 in Medford, Massachusetts, Pauline moved just a few years later with three siblings and a recently widowed mother to Wilmington.

Together they lived with Pauline's aunt, Alice Dunbar-Nelson, an educator and writer. Pauline's grandmother also lived in the household, so that the four children grew up under the supervision of three matriarchs.

Pauline graduated from Howard High School, an institution that would factor in her later career choice. Moreover, Howard functioned as the sole educational option for Wilmington's African American children.

Wilmington enforced strict segregation at the time. Numerous parks, restaurants, movie theaters, and other public gatherings prohibited Black patrons. Black Wilmingtonians established their own enclaves by offering venues otherwise denied to them. While Wilmington's hotels refused service, private homes welcomed scores of African American visitors, including notable Black celebrities. Both Pauline's mother and aunt taught and regularly hosted special lectures and other events at their home.

"Our home in Wilmington," Pauline later observed, "was a nice stopover place for people like James Weldon Johnson, Langston Hughes, or Paul Robeson. We used to listen to them talk as children. We never realized they were history makers." (cont. on pg. 99)

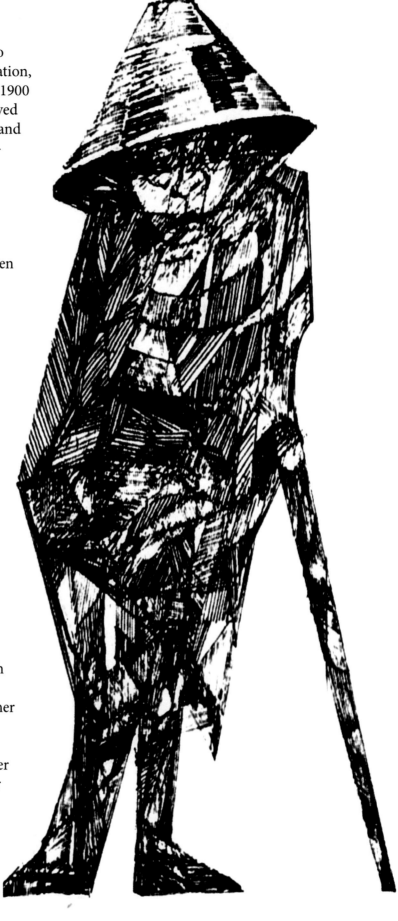

'The Curmudgeon,' by Dr. James E. Newton, a friend of Young's. "That's what she called herself," he said.

42

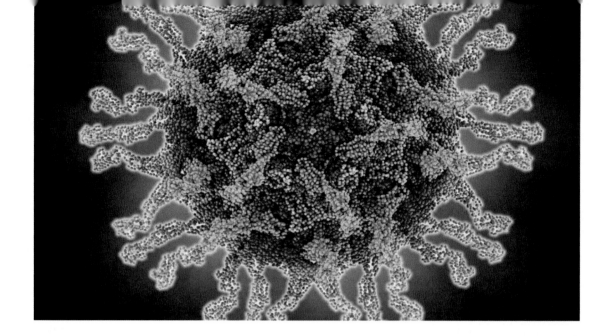

Polio Epidemic

"Do you remember Wilmington two years ago when the newspapers and the radios were blaring out polio headlines and when the public was almost hypnotized by the fear of the disease?" Local newspaper columnist Bill Frank was just warming up. "There's that classic story of a Wilmington couple who went vacationing in their cabin cruiser in 1947. They pulled up to a dock down in the South for refueling. They were told to move on—because someone on the dock had seen 'Wilmington' on the stern of the cruiser.

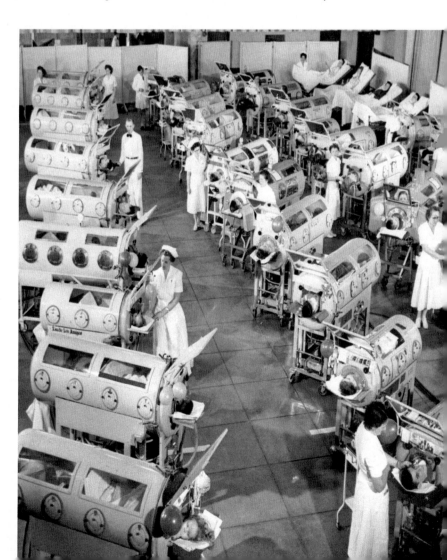

"The Wilmingtonians were told: 'You've got polio where you come from. Don't stop here.' Here at home, parents kept their children from the movies... canceled children's parties... and tried to keep the youngsters in a sort of a vacuum. The specter of fear really gripped the town." (cont. on pg. 100)

A new travel epoch along the Atlantic seaboard began on August 16, 1951, marking the opening of the Delaware Memorial Bridge. The 3,650 feet long (from anchorage to anchorage) crossing replaced the antiquated New Castle, Delaware—Pennsville Township, New Jersey Ferry, saving up to an hour's transit time. Now, vehicles on this graceful twin-suspension structure could soar high above the Delaware River.

Delaware shouldered the bulk of the cost, despite the bridge's clear benefit to New Jersey motorists. A historical anomaly resulted in the unique shape of the former's northern border, creating a distinctive 12-mile arc. This places both ends of the bridge within Delaware's authority. However, New Jersey built infrastructure leading to the bridge. Congressional approval was necessary for regional interstate highway designations.

One person stands out as the torch-bearer of this memorial bridge— Frank V. du Pont. (cont. on pg. 100)

THE DELAWARE MEMORIAL BRIDGE
CONTRACT #6
AMERICAN BRIDGE COMPANY
November 15, 1950

Historically Delaware's schools have been part of national struggles over educational inequality and segregation. Take the Supreme Court's 1896 *Plessy v. Ferguson* decree, for example. The decision affirmed the legality of racial segregation in public facilities under the "separate but equal" doctrine. The law held that segregation did not infringe upon the Equal Protection Clause in the Constitution's 14th Amendment, provided the separate facilities were of equal quality. The First State amended its constitution in 1897 to technically comply. Even so, the system perpetuated chronic inequality by underfunding Black community schools. The prevailing legal cornerstone of *Plessy v. Ferguson* shaped Delaware's school system well into the twentieth century. The National Association for the Advancement of Colored People (NAACP) sought to address the problem more forcefully. In a divided country, the organization harnessed legal challenges, grassroots activism, and policy advocacy to push towards true parity. (cont. on pg. 101)

Collins Seitz (left), a Chancery Court vice chancellor, and Louis Redding (above), a distinguished lawyer, were key figures in Delaware's fight against educational segregation. Through cases like Parker v. University of Delaware, *Seitz's judicial rulings and Redding's legal advocacy helped dismantle the "separate but equal" doctrine, paving the way for the landmark* Brown v. Board of Education *decision.*

Amish, Mennonites and Dunkards

Delaware became a haven in the early twentieth century for Anabaptist communities (Protestant Christian groups that believe in delaying baptism until the candidate confesses their faith in Christ, as opposed to doing so as infants.) The most prominent of these communities that came to Delaware were the Amish. Mennonites and Dunkards also settled in the state, although in far fewer numbers.

These denominations aim to harmonize tradition, community involvement, and spirituality in ways that strike most Americans as being from another era.

Amish families first settled in Delaware in 1915, having emigrated from McMinnville, Oregon. They traveled not by horse and buggy, but by train. According to Delaware historian Allen B. Clark, a community squabble likely drove their move. They were attracted to Kent County because of cheap land and fields of opportunity. (cont. on pg. 102)

Who would imagine a television station originating from an electrical company?

The Wilmington Electrical Specialty Company started a radio station in 1922 primarily to market radios, other electrical equipment, and engage potential customers. The new station, WHAV, debuted on July 22 as the first licensed in Delaware.

Wilmington Electrical Specialty changed the call letters to WDEL in 1926 to more accurately reflect the channel's Delaware origin.

The Lancaster, Pennsylvania media company Steinman Enterprises in 1947 purchased WDEL. Originally founded as a mining company, the family-owned firm had shifted over time to operate a newspaper chain.

The Steinmans' acquisition underscored their goal to diversify their print holdings. The purchase granted them entry to NBC's national-level radio programming. (cont. on pg. 104)

47

Mary Ann Wright, a Wilmington native, quietly ignited a groundbreaking movement in the late 1940s. She established Delaware's first non-profit for the physically and developmentally disabled. Named the Mancus Club, from the Latin for "maimed or crippled," her effort became a beacon of hope and resilience.

Wright (1920-2006), born with cerebral palsy, navigated life from a wheelchair. She was the first disabled individual to graduate from a Delaware public high school (1939). From there, Wright went on to begin a career as a licensed life insurance agent. She ultimately devoted 58 years to enhancing educational opportunities for the disabled, driven by compassion for others whose experience mirrored her own. (cont. on pg. 104)

Right: Nick Immediato, hamming it up on brother Hugo's shoulders, adds a finishing touch to a cake baked for a 1964 Mancus open house. Photo/Frank Fahey **Below:** *Mary Ann Wright (l) and Agnes Perrone*

48

Unions held a formidable position in Delaware as the 1950s blossomed. The post-World War II era ushered in a tremendous economic boom, one that reverberated across the nation. Jobs were abundant. Labor was in high demand. Unions saw an opportune moment to fortify their footing and wield greater bargaining power. By 1954, a substantial thirty-five percent of American workers had pledged their allegiance to the movement. Building on this momentum, John S. Turulski, a prominent Wilmington organizer, advocated for better wages and working conditions. (cont. on pg. 105)

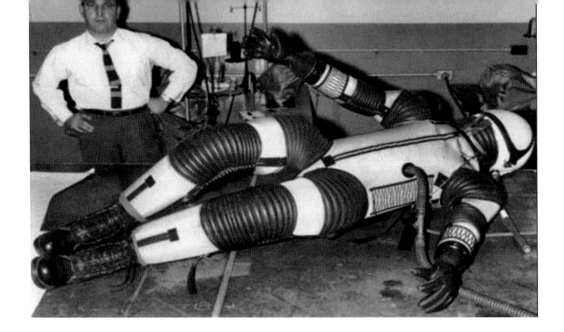

Neil Armstrong took mankind's first steps on the moon in a Delaware-designed and manufactured space suit. Armstrong had inched down the lunar module gingerly in July 1969, then radioed back to Houston ground control: "There seems to be no difficulty in moving around as we suspected. It's even perhaps easier than the simulations of one-sixth G [gravity] that we performed in the various simulations on the ground."

Crewmate Edwin "Buzz" Aldrin wasn't at all sure how stable the surface would be, or if it "would be like quicksand, literally sucking a person down into a quagmire of dust," as he wrote later.

Armstrong and Aldrin were wearing big, bulky space suits designed to protect them from intense cosmic radiation. ILC Dover's Model A-7L spacesuit was a highly specialized outfit with more than 24 different layers. Each one played a specific role, from temperature regulation to shielding astronauts against space's extremes. (cont. on pg. 106)

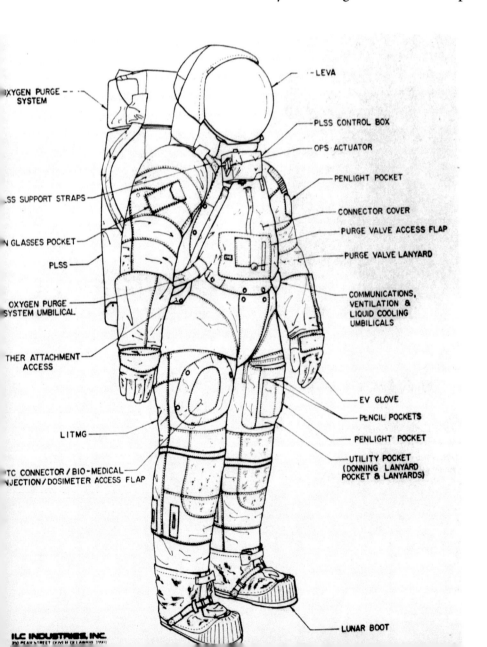

OXYGEN PURGE SYSTEM

SS SUPPORT STRAPS

N GLASSES POCKET

PLSS

OXYGEN PURGE SYSTEM UMBILICAL

THER ATTACHMENT ACCESS

LITMG

TC CONNECTOR / BIO-MEDICAL NJECTION / DOSIMETER ACCESS FLAP

LEVA

PLSS CONTROL BOX

OPS ACTUATOR

PENLIGHT POCKET

CONNECTOR COVER

PURGE VALVE ACCESS FLAP

PURGE VALVE LANYARD

COMMUNICATIONS, VENTILATION & LIQUID COOLING UMBILICALS

EV GLOVE

PENCIL POCKETS

PENLIGHT POCKET

UTILITY POCKET (DONNING LANYARD POCKET & LANYARDS)

LUNAR BOOT

ILC INDUSTRIES, INC.

Before the Beat Generation arrived, the sleepy fishing villages on the Delaware coastline were mere whispers of the vibrant travel destinations they would become. These towns, nestled quietly against the Atlantic, stood on the cusp of upheaval.

The allure of the open road, the ascension of fast food, and, most crucially, the cultural tidal wave brought forth by the Beat Generation all converged. Delaware's beach towns—previously known for their Methodist summertime camps and workaday waterfronts—started humming with a new and rebellious spirit. Rock and roll began to shake the foundations of American culture. (cont. on pg. 107)

51

Delaware State Parks acts as the custodian of over 13,000 acres of land, one of the most substantial landholders in the state, and the largest guardian of publicly owned land. The department also has the unique distinction of managing the highest number of historic structures inside Delaware's borders. This dual role converged within the Department of Natural Resources and Environmental Control starting in the 1960s.

Delaware Governor Richard McMullen enacted the State Park Commission in 1937, initiating the creation of parks, playgrounds, and preserves. But it was the 1960s that marked a milestone in Delaware's park history.

Eight of the existing seventeen state parks sprang to life during this decade. The confluence of three factors played a crucial role in this development. (cont. on pg. 108) ***Above:*** *Killens Pond State Park* ***Below:*** *Auburn Valley State Park*

The Civil Rights Act of 1964 sought to dismantle institutional racism and discrimination deeply ingrained in American society. The bill's sweeping focus aimed to eliminate barriers that perpetuated inequality against Black Americans. US legislators recognized the need to construct new legal foundations in a broader quest for equal rights. Congress proposed to ban segregation in public facilities, schools, and workplaces by outlawing unequal treatment based on race, color, religion, sex, or national origin.

Delaware's Senator J. Caleb "Cale" Boggs, who served from 1961 to 1972, played an active role in the collective passage of the act. He, like many of his Washington colleagues, felt pressured to tackle both Jim Crow institutionalization and the growing unrest stirred by the broad-based civil rights movement.

Boggs, Delaware's governor from 1953 to 1960, showed a commitment to civil rights. He set a precedent in education reform as the first chief executive of a segregated-school state to spearhead the implementation of 1954's *Brown v. Board of Education.* (cont. on pg. 109)

Sen. Cale Boggs on ladder

Delaware's efforts to democratize higher education for people of diverse income levels have resulted in such programs as today's SEED (Student Excellence Equals Degree) venture. The scholarship initiative offers tuition support to the state's high school graduates seeking higher education at select local institutions within commuting distance. (cont. on pg. 110)

Above: *The Delaware Technical & Community College opened its first campus in Georgetown in 1967, welcoming an inaugural class of 250-300 students to the "Southern Campus."*
Below: *Secretarial classes at the same campus, undated photo.*

Martha G. Bachman, educational advocate, possessed a spirit of volunteerism. She never was one to sit on the sidelines. "When I first started making suggestions to educators about ways to improve the system, they didn't take me seriously," she once reflected. "They told me I didn't know enough because I wasn't a professional. So I became a professional—a professional volunteer." Bachman, born in 1924 in Indianapolis, turned others' skepticism into the catalyst for her influential 37-year career.

Bachman traced her community organizer roots to 1945 when she helped establish the American School in Torreón, Mexico. "When we first moved to Mexico, I knew nothing about the language or the people there," she said. "Everything was a bit strange to say the least."

Bachman refused to be an observer. "I was one of 35 American parents who organized to form a first-rate school," the mother of four said. "The school was open to Americans and Mexicans alike. This showed me that the more people get involved, the more they can change things."

The DuPont Company relocated Louis Bachman, Sr. to Wilmington in 1954. Seizing this new opening, his wife became a volunteer teacher's aide at the Opportunity School for the Trainably Retarded in Marshallton. She devoted herself to the institution for six years, making herself an integral part of the learning facility. "I did whatever I could to help out at the school," she said. "I just like to work with young people — they are our tomorrow." (cont. on pg. 111)

Bombay Hook National Wildlife Refuge

Delaware Bay is one of the most important stopover sites in the Western Hemisphere for migratory shorebirds. During the late nineteenth and early twentieth centuries, untold numbers traversed the marshy wilds of Bombay Hook. Then, overhunting and creeping habitat loss caused precipitous declines in this unique flyway. The fashion industry's demand for trendy feathers even drove some species to the brink of extinction.

The haven sprawls over 15,000 acres, where the melodies of nature rhyme with every flutter and chirp. The incredible diversity of the sanctuary provides a striking scene, particularly during the spring and fall migrations. That is when many flocks of birds, including Canada geese and snow geese, find a crucial place to temporarily take a long journey's rest.

Their soft honks echo across the refuge as they glide over the brackish tidal marsh and prepare to land on freshwater ponds. This bi-annual ritual signals the coming of seasonal changes.

The geese, numbering between thirty and thirty-six thousand during the spring and fall peaks, contribute to the eastern route of North America's one-million-strong goose migration along the Atlantic Flyway. Snow Geese navigate using innate knowledge, environmental cues, and social learning from experienced flock members, ensuring their successful journey across vast distances. (cont. on pg. 112)

Edmund "Ted" Harvey was enchanted with saving wild habitats from an early age. He recalled his first encounter with creating a "greenprint" for conservation and development. "I saw the Great Pocomoke Swamp as a boy, and it was love at first sight," Harvey said in a late-life interview. "I knew then that these ecosystems needed protection from fragmentation." Ted Harvey was the son of Renee du Pont and LeRoy Harvey, Wilmington's mayor in the early 1920s. Young Harvey was also a nephew of T. Coleman du Pont, famous for the Dupont Highway. Tragically, both Renee and LeRoy passed away while Ted was still young. Lacking their guidance and direction, he found himself aimlessly wandering through a life of pleasure without responsibility. Harvey drifted down to the Florida Keys as a young adult. (cont. on pg. 113)

Above: *At 29, Ted Harvey saw the Florida Everglades ravaged by dredging and unregulated lumbering. Five years after this 1940 portrait, authorities established Everglades National Park to protect the area.*

Left: *Wildlife in Delaware's Great Cypress Swamp: carpenter frog, zebra swallowtail butterfly, prothonotary warbler.*

Below: The horseshoe crab is the Delaware State Marine Animal, a major beneficiary of the Coastal Zone Act. (Origami horseshoe crab shown here designed by Michael G. LaFosse, folded by Phillip West/ Flickr.) The Coastal Zone Act of 1971, a landmark in Delaware's environmental policy, aimed at protecting the state's 381-mile coastline from heavy industrialization. This legislation, championed by Governor Russell W. Peterson, reflected a period of growing ecological consciousness influenced by broader social movements. The law continues to stir controversy, symbolizing the ongoing struggle to balance natural world preservation with Delaware's economic growth. The Act shaped subsequent conservationist policies across the United States.

Seizing a historical moment, Peterson passionately campaigned to pass the Act under the banner "To hell with Shell," as the company sought to build a refinery along New Castle County's coast. The early 1970s marked a watershed for eco-activism, invigorated by broader social unrest. Governor Peterson took advantage of the growing public activism and protests around civil rights and the Vietnam War. (cont. on pg. 114)

Opposite Page: Delaware emerged unexpectedly during the tumultuous 1960s as a strong advocate for women's rights. This era, marked by social upheaval and activism, set the stage for a nationwide push towards gender equality.

Women faced pervasive discrimination in various aspects of life, from the workplace to social settings. Job listings were often segregated by gender, with higher-paying positions reserved for men. Women could legally be paid less than men for the same work and were often passed over for promotions. In some states, women could not serve on juries or obtain credit cards in their own names. Social norms relegated women to the domestic sphere, limiting their opportunities for personal and professional growth.

Betty Friedan's groundbreaking book, *The Feminine Mystique*, published in 1963, brought these issues to the forefront of public consciousness. (cont. on pg. 115)

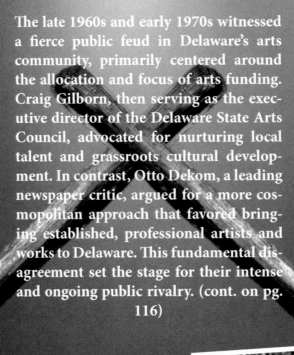

The late 1960s and early 1970s witnessed a fierce public feud in Delaware's arts community, primarily centered around the allocation and focus of arts funding. Craig Gilborn, then serving as the executive director of the Delaware State Arts Council, advocated for nurturing local talent and grassroots cultural development. In contrast, Otto Dekom, a leading newspaper critic, argued for a more cosmopolitan approach that favored bringing established, professional artists and works to Delaware. This fundamental disagreement set the stage for their intense and ongoing public rivalry. (cont. on pg. 116)

Did you know that the technology keeping you comfortable in the wilderness has a history as rich as the landscapes you explore?

Gore-Tex's
inception emerges
as a captivating story in
the development of manmade
fabrics. Wilbert Lee Gore, the founder
of W.L. Gore & Associates in Newark, teamed
up with his son Bob in a groundbreaking endeavor.
Together, they created what they thought to be the first-ever
instance of a breathable, waterproof material made from expanded
polytetrafluoroethylene (ePTFE). Wilbert and wife Genevieve had established W.L. Gore & Associates in 1958. Gore headed operations research for the
DuPont Company from 1945 till 1957. The Gores made their first product, an insulated
computer cable, in their Newark basement. "My father was an optimist, an enthusiastic optimist," said Bob Gore, the company's president from 1976 to 2000. (cont. on pg. 117)

Low-number License Plates

What is the curious allure of low Delaware license plate numbers? Their social symbolism defines the pecking order, extending beyond mere auto registration. This unique fascination is deeply ingrained in the state's history. These First State numbers are not just identifiers, but treasured assets.

Eye-catching low numbers powerfully proclaim "I'm a native," distinguishing long-standing residents from newcomers. Transferable and often passed down through generations, they hold a special place in family wills as prized heirlooms.

Single-digit plates have always been the most prized. The lowest-numbered plates indicate the governor, and proximity to those numbers suggests political influence. The crème de la crème—license plate No. 1—always adorns the limousine of the current governor, while No. 2 goes to the lieutenant governor and No. 3 to the secretary of state. You might see one, or all three, parked on Legislative Mall in Dover when elected officials are in session.

The cultural significance of these plates has given rise to a profitable local cottage industry centered around auctioning legacy auto registrations. (cont. on pg. 118)

Delaware, a cradle for distinguished individuals, includes figures who left an indelible mark. Their impact spans law, politics, social advocacy, and scholarship. Some have gone on to meaningfully shape national and international discourse. Among them is Joe Biden *(top left)*, a long-tenured senator celebrated for substantial legislative groundwork before serving as vice president and later president. Adding to this illustrious list is John Bassett Moore *(bottom left)*, a luminary in international law, and William V. Roth, Jr. *(middle right)*, the IRA maestro, who reformed fiscal and tax policy. Elise du Pont *(top right)* shines as a dedicated public servant with a flair for international diplomacy. Jeannette Eckman *(middle left)*, a pioneer in women's rights, and Muriel E. Gilman *(bottom right)*, a tireless advocate for the elderly and underserved, also find their names etched into the First State's history. (cont. on pg. 119)

The Nanticoke people have always been an integral part of Delaware's heritage. Historically known as skilled anglers, trappers, and farmers, the Nanticokes have navigated the challenges of maintaining their cultural identity amidst changing times. The remarkable story of the powwow showcases their steadfast perseverance in preserving their traditions.

"Many moccasins will make Millsboro the stamping grounds for Delaware's first Nanticoke Indian Pow Wow," proclaimed Wilmington's *News Journal* in 1978. This announcement did not capture the full context; the article overlooked the powwow's first non-native public presentation in 1922. Further decades of work laid the groundwork for the revitalized event.

The Nanticoke Indian Association first took root in 1921, spearheaded by Chief Wyniaco, also known as

William Russell Clark *(above with wife Florence)*. The association's basic purpose was to preserve the history, folklore, and culture of the Nanticokes. The chief's role transcended mere leadership. He embodied a vision for his people. (cont. on pg. 120)

Right: Redlining was a discriminatory practice where certain services were denied or unfavorably altered, usually in racially segregated areas. The 1930s Home Owners' Loan Corporation maps color-coded neighborhoods based on creditworthiness, solidifying redlining by marking some areas as high-risk, which led to long-term disinvestment. Below: 1950: World War II veteran Eugene Harris stands at his new home's entrance at 408 Rogers Road, Dunleith Estates, with Thomas H. Stillwell (Veterans Administration regional office manager), Don Loftus (builder of Dunleith), and James F. McDonough (VA loan guaranty officer) who facilitated the home financing.

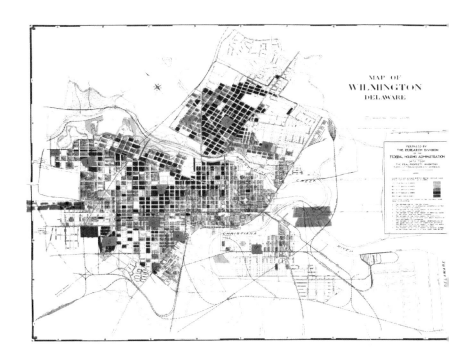

The Great Depression cast a long shadow over America, necessitating a major financial overhaul in housing. This period of domestic instability saw Congress respond with key institutions between 1932 and 1938, a venture which would shape the long-term residential market. They include a) the Federal Home Loan Bank System; b) the Home Owners' Loan Corporation; c) the Federal Housing Administration; and d) the Federal National Mortgage Association.

These programs helped Americans, for example, by providing mortgage insurance, thereby promoting affordable homeownership. The series of new financing programs, aimed at stabilizing the real estate sector, also aggravated racial segregation and economic disparity. This became evident through manipulations of FHA-backed loans and the discriminatory practice of redlining. (cont. on pg. 121)

generated by Dall-E

Left: Jack-o'-lanterns. Pie filling. Projectiles. The zany legacy of the Punkin Chunkin competition inspires the pumpkins of Delaware to dream of soaring through the sky. Post-Halloween, the gourds become a splatter of orange confetti on the horizon! An ordinary dispute between Trey Melson and Bill Thompson in 1986 transformed into something extraordinary. The pair debated who could devise a method to throw a pumpkin the farthest. Rather than ending the disagreement, they created the Punkin Chunkin competition. That year, the duo held the first-ever event with just three contestants and a handful of spectators.

This madcap rally brought together backyard engineers to test the limits of pumpkin physics. Beginning as a humble competition near Milton, the event's unique and thrilling nature led to skyrocketing popularity. Over the decades, the big launch left a notable mark on Bridgeville's social and cultural landscape. (cont. on pg. 122)

Below: The passage of the Financial Center Development Act (FCDA) in 1981 marked a decisive turn in Delaware's financial landscape. This legislation, championed by Governor Pierre "Pete" du Pont *(below)*, aimed to decontrol credit terms as well as invite out-of-state banks to set up shop in Delaware. Chase Manhattan and Morgan Guaranty Trust Co., two of the nation's banking behemoths, acted swiftly with the ink hardly dry on the FCDA. They pledged to open subsidiaries in Wilmington, igniting a spark that would soon fan into a financial flame. Delaware, embracing the FCDA, joined South Dakota in an exclusive club of states rolling out the red carpet for out-of-state banks. This move was not without detractors. Consumer groups raised the alarm, spearheaded by the Consumer Federation of America and supported by the Washington-based Center for the Study of Responsive Law. They expressed concern about added charges on credit transactions and the elimination of interest rate ceilings. "The bill may be good for Delaware in attracting more business," fumed James Boyle from the Federation, "but you are acting to supersede the laws of many other states." Despite these concerns, the wheels of financial change were already in motion. As the 1980s progressed, the promise of a well-positioned Delaware banking sector began to materialize. The development saw an increasing number of banks set up local branches and growing financial industry employment opportunities. (cont. on pg. 123)

The dawn skies above Delaware Bay come alive during the spring and fall migration seasons. Birds in transit flock to crowded shores, a habitat both precious and precarious. This 134-mile natural marvel has long drawn attention and mirrors the broader ecological importance of estuaries.

The Atlantic Flyway exemplifies this symbiotic relationship between mankind and nature. The vast 1.1 million acres of wetlands are among the state's most precious natural resources. The area is the second-largest staging area in North America for migratory shorebirds and home to many endangered species.

The Delaware Bay narrative, however, is tinged with caution. Economic pressures regularly resurface, raising the issue of the coastal zone's potential industrialization. Time and again, humanity must steward these invaluable regional aquatic ecosystems responsibly for the benefit of future generations. (cont. on pg. 124)

Sussex County underwent a meaningful demographic shift from 1990 to 2000. A surge in the Hispanic population primarily drove this ten-year change. This evolution came as a surprise to a community more familiar with people leaving than new cultures arriving. Long-time residents elicited mixed responses. Data indicate that as the Hispanic population rose, non-Hispanic residents moved out.

Seasonal workers have long been part of Sussex County's social fabric. The new wave of Hispanics was mostly male and typically lived near poultry processing plants. Communities such as Selbyville, Georgetown, and Milford experienced particularly notable population increases.

The 1990 census found that the Bridgeville/Greenwood area had the largest Hispanic population increase in Sussex County, growing from 64 to 225. Maximino Alcantara, 20 years of age, said he liked Delaware "because here I go to work." Most of his Mexican housemates, all men, all from Chontalpa, worked in the poultry plants of southern Delaware and Maryland. They made the rounds, said Alcantara, the only one who spoke English. They shifted from Allen Family Foods to Perdue to ConAgra Poultry, earning between $6 and $7 an hour. They went back to Mexico around Christmas and when they returned, worked at whichever plant had openings. (cont. on pg. 125)

Left: *The northern tip of Brandywine Creek Valley is an essential part of the Du Pont legacy known as 'Chateau Country', with Pennsylvania's Longwood Gardens (left) as but one notable feature. The region also hosts the esteemed Winterthur and Nemours estates, Delaware's most visited. Longwood Gardens, a nearby horticultural wonder, along with the other two estates, captivate with botanical beauty, offering seasonal displays year-round. Longwood nurtures 4,600 varieties of plants and trees across 1,077 acres. Once home to 50 du Pont estates, Brandywine Creek Valley now has 15, each adding to the aristocratic narrative that defines Chateau Country.*

Delaware introduced critical reforms in the state's approach to tourism during the last quarter of the twentieth century. The state, known primarily as a beach destination, needed to diversify visitor appeal. Sightseeing had become the state's second-largest industry by the close of this period. Visitors spent $223 million in Delaware in 1975 alone. These robust figures spurred the state to adopt a multifaceted strategy to capitalize on this vital emergence. In 1973, the Division of Economic Development founded the Delaware State Travel Service (DSTS). However, this new offshoot did not receive appreciable support. The service initially had only two staff members and operated on a limited budget.

DSTS director Donald R. Mathewson encountered difficulties in renovating Delaware's travel industry. "We've estimated that the average daytime visitor spends about 6.64 hours in the state," he said. "During the peak summer season he tailgates his way to the beaches in Sussex County, goes for a swim, buys his kid an orange soda on the boardwalk and drives home." (cont. on pg. 126)

Four Wilmington community leaders emerged in the late twentieth century as beacons of social change. Father Roberto Balducelli, an Oblate of Saint Francis de Sales priest, led St. Anthony of Padua parish for three decades from 1959, where he established key mission projects. Brother Ronald Giannone founded Delmarva's first emergency shelter *(right)* in 1977. Sister Jeanne Cashman transitioned to social welfare in 1987, founding Sojourner's Place. Reverend Maurice Moyer *(above)*, at Community Presbyterian Church since 1955, became a vital figure in the civil rights movement. Each, in their own way, built a sanctuary of community support, activism, and moral guidance. (cont. on pg. 127)

Digital Medical Technology

The digital revolution swept through Delaware like a tidal wave, leaving no industry untouched. Healthcare was no exception. Cutting-edge technologies like computed tomography (CT) and magnetic resonance imaging (MRI) changed how hospitals, clinics, and physician practices diagnosed patients. While such sophisticated scanning equipment was out of reach for many providers, the emergence of specialized medical diagnostic imaging centers (MDICs) provided a more affordable alternative. These independent, private facilities offered dedicated radiographic services and advanced visualization for a fraction of the cost.

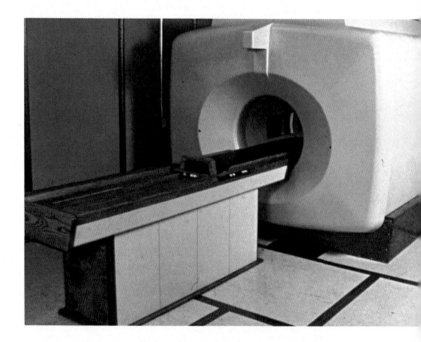

Hospital systems and individual physician or specialist practices often chose to refer patients to these centers instead of incurring substantial expenses themselves. This approach allowed for more cost-effective access to advanced diagnostic tools. Standalone MDICs proved a viable complementary model, accelerating the proliferation of new scanning technologies. (cont. on pg. 128)

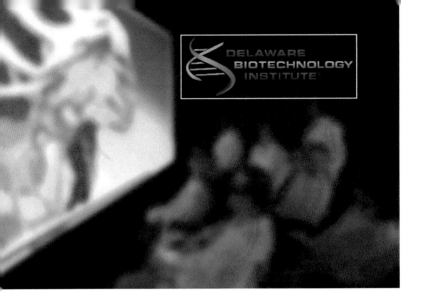

Governor Tom Carper had a vision to bolster Delaware's scientific prowess as the new millennium approached. He earmarked $10 million in his 2000 budget for the formation of the Delaware Biotechnology Institute (DBI). Carper stated that the center would help in "creating and retaining jobs in biotechnology, sharing research and development costs among companies, and providing educational opportunities for students."

DBI architects fostered five partnerships among Delaware research organizations. These included the University of Delaware, Delaware State University, Christiana Care Health System, Nemours/ AI DuPont Hospital for Children, and Delaware Technical and Community College.

This ambitious initiative aimed to push the state toward the global biotechnological frontier. Delaware academia, local corporations, and the broader scientific community would be equipped to nurture a fruitful symbiotic relationship.

The consortium established a base facility nestled within the University of Delaware. David Weir *(shown here middle photo)* assumed the helm as founding director. He held a doctorate in chemical physics and lectured at the University of St. Andrews in Scotland early in his career. (cont. on pg. 128)

Dr. Ulysses Samuel Washington's illustrious academic career speaks volumes about unwavering dedication. Dr. Washington's 44 years of employment at Delaware State University included terms as professor and chair of the Department of Agriculture, extension administrator, research director, interim athletic director, interim head football coach, assistant football coach, acting director of Conwell Hall, and director of the recreation demonstration program under Title III. He is also remembered as a fixture at DSU's commencement exercises, where he served as chief marshal for over four decades.

U.S. Washington was born July 16, 1920 in Dilwyn, Virginia, the second of eight children. "Wash" attended public elementary and high school in that small Buckingham County town before beginning his secondary studies at Saint Paul's Junior College. He transferred to Virginia State College (now University), where in 1942 he earned a bachelor's degree in agriculture, playing basketball at both schools. While at VSC, the running guard earned honorable mention at the Central Intercollegiate Athletic Association Conference. Washington's coaching career began at Manassas Regional High School, where he led the football team for two years. The newly minted teacher also taught agriculture there before reporting for naval duty in World War II.

Following his honorable discharge, Washington detoured into the family's sawmill business. (cont. on pg. 129)

Above: *Dr. Washington works with two students at Delaware State's College of Agriculture greenhouse, mid-1970s.*

The evolution of the internet, a cornerstone of modern life, can be traced back to numerous pioneers with visionary ideas. Their relentless endeavors over decades have reshaped the way we interact, work, and learn.

Three individuals associated with the University of Delaware hold noteworthy places among those innovators. Each one has made distinct contributions.

David J. Farber came to prominence in the late 1970s after earning a master's degree in mathematics from the Stevens Institute of Technology. *Wired* magazine called him "the Paul Revere of the Digital Revolution." Farber began his professional career at Bell Laboratories. He was part of the team that invented the first electronic telephone switch. Additionally, he contributed to the creation of the computer language SNOBOL.

Farber's trajectory led him to the University of Delaware. There, he played a critical role in developing CSNet. This multinodal network connected computer science departments across roughly 500 colleges and universities. "Delaware was the central hub in the early days of networking," Farber reflected. "You didn't talk to anyone in the academic world without going through Delaware."

Farber laid the groundwork for scholarly collaboration. (cont. on pg. 130)

Notes on Photographs

Page 8 Reedbirds

Wilmington's *Evening Journal* in 1907 painted a vivid picture of marshes teeming with them. They sought the First State's plentiful natural barriers for wildlife shelters. Gunners flooded the grainfields and meadows as a "miniature battle" of shots erupted to claim the prized birds.

"It is toward sunset," the *Journal* continued, "and the weather is fine, that the sport of shooting Reed birds is most profitable. They resort to the borders of the rivers and estuaries to roost, where they pick up grubs and insects found at the roots of the blades."

The *Morning News* reported on September 1, 1908, that the reedbird season had commenced, promising a plentiful hunt "in quest of the toothsome reedbird."

Dolichonyx oryzivorus was also nicknamed the "rice-bird" due to a predictable habit of feasting on cultivated rice in the Carolinas while migrating en route to South America.

"For so long a time that the memory of man runs not to the contrary, the reedbirds have been to the rice planters a plague comparable to that of the storied locusts, but with this difference, that they arrive not once in a while but every year, and inevitably," reported the *New York Sun* southern correspondent in 1915.

"So enormous are their numbers and so insatiable their appetite that it becomes a question whether the bird or the planter shall gather the crop. The only way to save the latter is to wage an unceasing war against the birds, and for a full month of days it is the principal business of every man woman and child to bang away with a shotgun at the feathered predators."

Hunting reedbirds, whether for food or pest control, would soon encounter legislative hurdles. Conservation activists, alarmed at dwindling bird populations, instigated the Migratory Bird Treaty Act of 1918. The legislation aimed to protect a myriad of migrating birds, thereby nurturing a broader ecological equilibrium.

Delaware's Senator Willard Hickman and Governor Charles Miller found themselves at odds with this federal law. They strongly felt the decree conflicted with Delaware's pre-existing game laws and thereby cut into hunting-related revenues. Yet Congress turned a deaf ear and went on to pass the new statute.

Southern rice growers were furious. The Migratory Bird Act threatened their very livelihoods. They pressured Woodrow Wilson's Secretary of Agriculture, David Houston, to declare the birds "detrimental to their agricultural interests." Houston yielded to their demands. In January 1919, less than six months after the restriction had first been enacted, he authorized eight southern states, along with Delaware, to lift the reedbird hunting ban.

But the exemption did not endure. The USDA withdrew the allowance in March 1927, due to declining bird populations. The reedbirds once again came under federal protection.

This intricate tale highlights the transitions in a species' public perception. Initially a culinary staple in Delaware, the reedbird was deemed a Deep South agricultural nuisance. The bobolink over time garnered federal protection. The story reveals the interplay between local customs and national interests. *lithograph by John Jay Audubon, The New York Public Library collection*

Page 9 Seaford Library

The Acorn Club's passion for the Free Public Library grew, and so did their activities: readings, lectures, chamber music and high teas.

President Mabel Read reported that by May, the library had grown to 300 volumes. The Society began to print a broadsheet called "The Great Oak" to stay in the public eye.

Such spirited community engagement both generated funds as well fostered a sense of ownership and pride. In 1909 the new president, Mrs. E. Greenabaum, proudly stated that "the club has taken the town library under its auspices."

This growth reflected a turning point for the Acorn Club. Mrs. Thomas Rawlins' 1910 election to president brought much-needed statewide donor connections. She had wielded an influential role in the Delaware State Federation of Women's Clubs as state chairman for libraries and literature. The Acorn Club, alongside the library, relocated in 1910 to a more spacious venue within the historic Henry White building, situated at the corner of Pine and King Streets, merely a few blocks from Seaford's Nanticoke River docks.

Rawlins declared that both the Acorn Club and the Federation "are deeply interested in better library conditions in all Delaware towns and in addressing the problems of wholesome amusement for young people." Close friends with Emily P. Bissell, Christmas Seals fund-raiser extraordinaire, Rawlins promptly leveraged Bissell's philanthropic network.

Rawlins aimed to better reach book lovers in outlying areas by sending Sussex County's first bookmobile. She authorized Mary Hopkins, a State Traveling Library Commission member, to purchase a library car in 1912. Mary headed out, vehicle seats stacked high, to visit nearby farms, loaning books as she went. Within four years, Hopkins managed five bookmobiles in a sprawling county territory.

The Acorn Club committed itself to ensuring central library access at times convenient for the surrounding communities. The members' dedication kept the facility open on Saturday afternoons from 1915 onward, catering to rural folks who came into town for shopping, socializing, and sharing the week's news.

The Seaford Library's holdings swelled in 1916 to more than 1,200 books. Serious donors noticed. Mr. and Mrs. Willard Morse, for example, presented leatherbound editions of Thackeray's complete works, all 15 volumes. Additionally, this couple provided a five-book edition of *The Rise of the Dutch Republic*. Other major collectors followed. Subsequent bequests further elevated the library's reputation.

These substantial contributions, along with the dedicated Acorn Club efforts, transformed the Seaford Library into an institution that was ready to stand on its own. Three decades in, the premises could no longer be considered a hole in the wall.

In response to the growth, library administrators chose to separate from the Acorn Club in 1932. The Seaford Library Commission over-saw the new, independent organization. Nonetheless, the club continued to donate money for seven years to the dream members had fought so hard to establish. These ambitious Seaford women sowed the seed of intellectual enrichment, watching their sprout grow into a mighty oak. Such diligence underscores a timeless truth: from modest beginnings, great things may come. *photo courtesy Delaware Public Archives/Harold W. T. Purnell Photograph Collection*

Page 10 Wilmington Trust Company

The du Ponts reviewed the company's banker agreements for arrangements that put the organization at a disadvantage. In response, they founded Wilmington Trust Company, securing a controlling interest, to prevent future negotiations from hindering their ambitions.

Coleman and Pierre du Pont founded their institution just one month after the 1899 General Corporation Law made the state an attractive hub for liberal corporate registrations. The determined du Ponts wanted a piece of both the new business, plus associated banking needs. Although Alfred du Pont served on the Wilmington Trust Company board, he was not hands-on in day-to-day management.

The du Ponts made a calculated decision, believing they had something unique to offer businesses similarly complex to their interests. Wilmington Trust's staff, seasoned by work for DuPont Corporation, could be counted on to offer a level of unparalleled sophistication. This expertise was predicted to draw large corporate clients to Delaware from far and wide. Their gamble worked.

Wilmington Trust began conducting business on July 8, 1903, in the first constructed section of the DuPont building campus. The three cousins debated over the name for the block-wide complex.

Alfred, the idealist, proposed honoring family ancestors by naming it the "du Pont de Nemours Building." Coleman, the most pragmatic of the three, suggested shortening the name to "the DuPont Building," arguing the public would call the structure that anyway.

Pierre, the most attuned to the banking sector, suggested naming the hub the "Wilmington Trust Company Building." He believed that associating the 1907 complex with the subsidiary's name would allow them to leverage the du Pont reputation. This strategy, in his esti-mation, would effectively advertise the family's growing banking sector.

It is no accident that Delaware's ascent as a global nexus for business formation began during this decade, and under their leadership. Legislators in Delaware were already embracing company-friendly policies, including chartering laws with low fees and high secrecy. 1907 General Corporation Law amendments further facilitated an advantageous business environment. Wilmington Trust rose to be-come the state's largest bank in 1912, a position the business held for over 100 years.

Delaware has emerged as the corporate capital of America for a reason. A proven century-old record of accomplishment has created a stable and appealing domicile for business registries. Flourishing corporate entities reflect the First State's enterprise-friendly governance. *Photo of Coleman du Pont: Bain News Service - Library of Congress; Photo of Pierre du Pont: Hagley Museum and Library Digital Archives, P.S. du Pont Longwood photograph collection; Photo of Alfred Du Pont: Hagley Museum and Library Digital Archives; court interior photo: The Delaware Supreme Court (State of Delaware)*

Page 11 Smyrna Opera House

The Guy Brothers Famous Minstrels wrapped up the decade with a vibrant traveling show. Smyrna High School regularly held com mencement exercises in the spacious hall, filling the chamber with energy. 1910 valedictorian Katherine Mannon waxed poetic on the "Quest of the Holy Grail." Ah, the timeless academic tradition of newly-minted graduates speechifying in pursuit of lofty ambitions.

The advent of Hollywood in the mid-1910s brought a subtle reshaping to the opera house's role. The playhouse was on the verge of becoming solely an entertainment venue, now poised to host live events and movie screenings. Displaying photoplays such as "Island of Regeneration" and "The Clause in the Constitution" became a part of the new identity.

The frequency of participatory gatherings began to wane in the early 1920s. Modern movie theaters had sprung up within reach of downtown Smyrna by the following decade, driving fierce competition.

The Smyrna Town Council and the local businessmen's association recognized the need to adapt. They explored potential renovations in late 1930 to transition into a more contemporary facility.

Competitor Benjamin Shindler controlled the Strand Theatre on nearby W. Commerce St. He had already been moving ahead on refurbishing his building to provide a fresh cinematic experience. His speed forced the opera house into a defensive position. The Town Council picked up the pace on modernizing their complex. Shindler completed his updates in November 1931, building two movie theaters in the space where there had been one.

A month later, the Como Theatre, or "People's Theatre," opened in the opera house. The venue, "for many years the pride of Smyrna people," said the *Evening Journal*, had been thoroughly upgraded. "A new velour curtain has taken the place of the old paper curtain." Opening night featured the Marx Brothers' "Monkey Business." Como owners recruited a Mr. Stewart, who had been Strand manager.

Competitive county-wide pressure mounted on downtown theatres. Smyrna moviegoers gained options as the family car transitioned from luxury to commonplace. A 20-minute drive one way led to Middletown's Everett Theatre (1922), and a 20-minute drive in the other direction brought film fans to Dover's Capitol Theatre (1923).

Richard M. Hollingshead built America's first drive-in theater in 1933, in Camden, New Jersey. Suddenly people could flock to open fields and watch movies from the comfort of their cars—no need to travel downtown anymore, where parking was sure to be a headache. The concept quickly gained popularity. City center halls felt the squeeze.

Meanwhile, the Como Theatre soldiered on for several more years. Then, in September 1936, an arsonist attacked. Smoke forced the movie house's closure. Between a Depression-battered economy and pressures from nearby town cinemas and drive-ins, there was little incentive to invest in a stagnating downtown. Consequently, the owners chose to walk away rather than rebuild. For the next 12 years, the once-elegant space lay dormant.

Post-World War II suburban movie houses, larger and more numerous, sprang up in fields surrounding Smyrna. Unconstrained by cramped downtown lots, they could offer expanded screens, more seating, parking, and spacious lobbies with better snack options.

Smyrna Opera House photo courtesy Delaware Public Archives

Page 12 Delaware Idioms

Commonplace language often strays from textbook rules, such as using "bottle of sweet smeller" instead of "perfume," or modifying "waistcoat" to "weskit," illustrating the progression from poor enunciation to locally accepted usage.

Delaware's exclamatory utterances, like "By granny!" and "I declare to kings!" form their own subset of idioms. Both minced oaths allow strong emotions to be expressed while maintaining decorum.

Some traditional dictums can trace their lineage to literary sources before eventually becoming common parlance. The word "druthers," for instance, is a linguistic retooling of "I'd rather." The new version inserted itself into everyday Delaware language thanks to widely read American writer Bret Harte, who in 1875 penned "drathers."

Agricultural life has undeniably left its mark on the First State's local dialect. Take "gee-hoppled," an early twentieth century turn-of-phrase referring to an off-balance individual. This description draws upon "gee and haw," a command to guide horses, and "hopple," a device to constrain a milking cow from kicking. "Dressed in his dismals" evocatively describes a farmer in knee-patched work clothes.

Delaware's dawn-of-the-twentieth-century figures of speech have persevered, some continuing in use today. "Honey," for example, a spousal term of endearment, sweetens many a Delaware home. Time's passage reflects a unique linguistic heritage.

Page 13 First Skyscraper

The Equitable and Ford Buildings had led a progressive construction tide through Wilmington's downtown, a wave of change between 5th and 11th Streets on Market.

Newer architectural features continued to redefine the skyline. This inventive surge heralded the advent of three modern technologies, each of which later became standard: steel framing, safety elevators, and central steam heating.

The Baynard and the Crosby & Hill buildings (one constructed in 1883, the other in 1888) were among Wilmington's early adopters of the steel-frame design. Located one block apart on Market Street, at the 5th and 6th Street intersections respectively, these towers highlighted the emerging architectural trend. Additionally, the two used the safety elevator, an invention that first appeared in New York City's Equitable Life Building (1870).

The Wilmington Savings Fund Society's 1886 edifice also unveiled these newest advancements. Philadelphia architect Addison Hutton designed a two-story, cathedral-style Gothic Revival building. He artfully combined cutting-edge techniques with a traditional castle-like appearance, concealing a robust iron-and-steel frame skeleton behind the heavy stone façade. Located at 9th and Market Street, Wilmington Savings incorporated central steam heating with effective floor-to-floor distribution.

This trio of framing, heating, and elevator advancements helped lay the groundwork for the creation of dramatically taller structures. The trailblazing towers exemplify a seminal period in Wilmington's architectural history. *Photo of Equitable Guarantee and Trust Company building courtesy of the Delaware Historical Society; photo of DuPont Building construction courtesy Hagley Library & Museum*

Page 14 Delaware Art Museum

A committed group of artists, led by Frank E. Schoonover, N. C. Wyeth, and Henry J. Pack, immersed themselves in preparations for the impending event. "The selection and installation committee started their work this morning," the *News Journal* reported on November 5. "Under their supervision, the canvas supports for the artworks were erected, and the process of arranging the pieces commenced."

November 12 finally arrived. The DuPont Building's Italian-marbled auditorium blossomed into a vibrant venue, one filled with the buzz of excitement for preserving vital history. Society notables, artists, and their friends, adorned in pearls and black-tie attire, gathered beneath the gleaming crystal chandeliers. "Like all private views there was as much interest in each other among the guests as there was in the pictures," winked the *Morning News*.

Amid the regalia of the du Ponts, Bayards, Bissells, Ridgelys, and Tallmans, the milieu was indeed an illustrious affair. Nonetheless, the true stars of the show, the 150 artworks, commanded everyone's mostly undivided attention.

The doors swung open the following day, marking a moment the city's residents had long anticipated. "Judging from the first day, the exhibition is going to be one of the most successful affairs ever held in the city," glowed the *Morning News*.

Daily afternoon teas added a touch of elegance to the occasion. They were hosted by various patronesses, including Pyle's daughters Phoebe and Eleanor. Wilmington's society pages highlighted the genteel fashions on display. Miss Phoebe wore a black crêpe dress paneled in royal blue, while Miss Eleanor sported one in brown velveteen, accented with yellow cording around the lapel.

Miss Jessie Wilson, daughter of President-elect Woodrow Wilson, stopped by on November 13, bringing an additional sense of prestige. Her presence at the afternoon tea hosted by Miss Ellen du Pont electrified the atmosphere.

Several pieces stood out as highlights at the heart of the exhibition. One notable work was "The Dancing Girl," a creation by Gayle P. Hoskins. This painting demonstrated his exceptional draftsmanship and lively color palette. Another piece, "A Portrait of Mrs. W.," captivated many viewers. Howard Pyle's widow had lovingly crafted this painting while summering on Cape Cod. Her husband's renowned piece, "Marooned," occupied a place of honor at center stage. Adorned with a green wreath tied with a purple ribbon, this touching homage to the departed artist added a poignant note.

The show, running until November 18, left an indelible impression on all who attended. Once the curtain fell, the event's artistic success became clear. Organizers felt the occasion had propelled Wilmington to a position among the nation's foremost art centers.

The exhibition laid the groundwork for the Delaware Art Museum, the state's largest fine art venue. Today this repository's worldwide collection boasts over 12,000 works. Howard Pyle would be proud. *Dupont Building interior: Hagley Museum and Library; "Marooned" painting courtesy Delaware Art Museum*

Page 15 DuPont Highway

The new State Highway Department would then maintain the road indefinitely, including bridge and culvert upkeep. Instead of granting any individual or group authority over any highway, the Act provided a pathway for backers to undertake more regional projects.

The Act empowered du Pont to found the DuPont Boulevard Corporation, serving as a conduit to realize his expansive vision. This engineer's foresight culminated in the eponymous route's innovative design and many safety features, all serving the purpose of establishing a new standard in roadway construction. The newly formed corporation, staffed by men of integrity, pledged to build enduring roads.

Such a bold project was bound to encounter resistance. Sure enough, the not-in-my-backyard (NIMBY) protesters materialized in New Castle County within days of the announcement of the plans.

The town of Arden objected to having the highway run so close to their village. "Tramps would follow the course of the smooth boulevard rather than the present rough highway, and the peace and quiet of Arden would be disturbed," reported the *Morning News*.

Wilmington detractors argued that the boulevard would necessitate additional policing, increase the cost of their city governance, and risk a heightened volume of accidents.

This NIMBY attitude compounded the challenges of securing rights-of-way in both New Castle and Kent Counties. The group, instead, found themselves compelled to commence work in Sussex County. Crews began construction in Georgetown on January 24, 1912.

Despite facing such relentless headwinds, du Pont and his associates exhibited remarkable courage and patience. In 1915, DuPont Boulevard Corporation successfully completed a twenty-mile stretch, from the town of Delmar on the Maryland line to Georgetown. The organization conveyed the road to the state.

A section of the road between Georgetown and Milford remained incomplete for four years. The Appenzeller Farm, south of Milford, put up fierce resistance and instigated continuous legal actions to prevent their land holdings from being cut in half.

The Boulevard Corporation in September 1917 proposed that the newly formed State Highway Department integrate the completed pavement into the larger emerging state road system. The General Assembly agreed.

The already completed twenty-mile concrete road in Sussex demonstrated to every Delaware business owner and farmer the potential value of a state-long connector.

The transfer came with three conditions: (1) The state agreed to the Boulevard's construction from Appenzeller Farm to Milford according to the pre-established plan; (2) the trunkline from Milford to Wilmington would proceed based on existing blueprints; and (3) these two projects would be the first to be completed by the Department.

Du Pont remained committed to the venture despite several years of labor shortages, economic disruption, and legislative delays related to the outbreak of World War I. He agreed to cover all trunkline costs, which in turn freed the state's road funds.

T. Coleman du Pont's pride and joy transformed the region into a vibrant tourist destination. The improved sightseeing access to those from northern Delaware and adjacent portions of the northeast spurred the development of area beaches.

Furthermore, southern Delaware blossomed into a major truck farming region, leveraging the improved access to urban centers. This shift in agricultural fundamentals allowed Sussex and Kent County farmers to market fruits, vegetables, and broiler chickens directly to northern consumers. This evolution ultimately reduced the region's reliance on railroads for transport.

DuPont Boulevard's design accommodated future high-speed, large-volume traffic. T. Coleman du Pont's visionary standards featured a 200-foot-wide right-of-way along with curves and grades suitable for fast-moving transportation. These early norms became a benchmark for modern highway design.

Du Pont's financial contribution to Delaware highway construction has never been matched. He paid $2,600,000 for a 75-mile stretch, equivalent to $783 million today.

DuPont Boulevard, eventually known as DuPont Highway (Route 13), laid a progressive foundation for building modern infrastructure. Numerous branching roads form an intricate network of connectivity. Furthermore, du Pont's influence transcended Delaware's borders. The new highway project built momentum for a broader regional transportation system. *Line drawing of fast car public domain; Pouring concrete photo Delaware Public Archives*

Page 16 Holly Industry

Twelfth-Night festivities in our corner of America culminated in the grand bonfire of January 6th, as the old year tipped a hat to the new one. The sweet-scented smoke from burning holly, evergreens, and mistletoe mingled with the experience of an icy starlit night.

One must journey back to the 1920s, a booming decade for this enterprise, to truly appreciate the holly wreath industry. A 1927 report to the General Assembly from the Commission for the Conservation of Forests paints a vivid picture of the industry's practices.

The business thrived mainly in Kent and Sussex counties. While holly grows statewide, the tree flourishes mostly in the deep woods, swamps, and moist depressions of these counties.

The industry was incredibly productive, annually shipping an estimated 7,000 cases (1.5 million wreaths) plus an additional 600 cases of loose sprays and branches. The annual net profit of $400,000 was a substantial boost to the agricultural economy.

W.B. Truitt launched a holly and pine packing/shipping business as early as 1905 in Millsboro. By the onset of World War II, this venture had become successful enough to emerge as a leading force in the state's holly wreath industry. Furthermore, the town carved out a niche for itself as one of the nation's primary holly wreath manufacturing and shipping hubs.

During November and December, surrounding area locals brought finished wreaths (which fetched 10-30 cents each from wholesalers), plus loose greens, to a facility located alongside the tracks of a Pennsylvania Railroad spur. Workers packed the greenery into wooden boxes, ready for prompt shipment by train and truck.

The rush was over for another year by the end of the Christmas season. The holly wreath business enabled many area families to abundantly celebrate the mistletoe tradition as well.

In the mid-1950s, the Department of Labor ruled that wreath makers were laborers and had to be paid by the hour, rather than piecework. This new regulation deterred many shippers from continuing in the occupation because they lacked the means to verify the time workers claimed they spent constructing a wreath.

The industry faced other challenges. First, holly collectors often cut down entire trees rather than just selectively pruning the branches, thereby killing off their groves. Second, the long-term sustainability of Delaware's holly industry was threatened by competition from states further south with bigger stands of trees.

Finally, as the mid-twentieth century unfolded, the advent of cheap and lifelike plastic holly wreaths started to gain ground. This development cast a shadow over Delaware's native holly industry. From the 1950s onwards, these low-maintenance artificial alternatives became increasingly popular, ultimately replacing the live holly wreathes once produced by Delaware families and industries. *Holly packing house photo Delaware Public Archives; "From the Land of Holly" graphic: public domain*

Page 17 World War I Munitions Support

Despite the utmost importance of safety in Bethlehem Loading's dangerous production, accidents still occurred. On July 26, 1918, a ten-inch shell exploded while being loaded, killing two men and injuring one. The reverberation was felt from a considerable distance.

Bethlehem Steel, conscious of their role, intensified their recruitment efforts in October. Their objective was clear: to ensure a steady supply of munitions to the American Expeditionary Forces under General John J. Pershing in World War I. "The Bethlehem Loading Company wants more workers to keep shells going to Pershing's men and appeals to all Delawareans for help," said the *Morning News*.

To this end, the company offered to transport any willing Delawarean from any town in the state to the munition plant in New Castle, using a special train running from Harrington north along the Pennsylvania Railroad, free of charge. This initiative underscored the critical link between domestic industrial capacity and the success of American forces on the European front, rallying community support for a cause seen as essential to the Allied victory effort.

Jobs were plentiful at Bethlehem Loading, offering better wages than those on the farms. Many citizens heeded the call. Smyrna's response typified this trend: "Thirty or more persons from Smyrna have answered the appeal of the government and accepted positions at the Bethlehem Loading Company plant at New Castle."

The firm's aggressive recruitment stirred resentment from downstate employers. In response, Assistant Superintendent Dunn offered a solution. "While the plant is in imperiled need of munition workers," he said, "if any community will certify that this train has taken labor from farms to any other essential industry, such laborers will be dismissed at once for the benefit of such downstate industries."

The war's end in 1918 brought a new set of challenges to New Castle. The once-constant demand for munitions plummeted and many wartime industries confronted an uncertain future. "The Bethlehem Loading Company plant below New Castle, shut down permanently at 6 o'clock this evening..." noted February 19, 1919 records. "The shutting down of this plant furlows about 500 employees."

Hopes for Bethlehem Loading's revival persisted even after the closure. The *News Journal* speculated in May on the plant's potential repurposing as a chemical manufacturing works. Tongues wagged about site reactivation for a Navy contract continued through June.

However, by September 1919, the lack of the facility's long-term viability became clear. Bethlehem Steel put the subsidiary up for sale. No

82

buyers came forward.

The once-bustling Bethlehem Loading Plant decayed into obscurity over the next six years. Bethlehem Steel finally dissolved the corporate entity. Delaware Rayon Company purchased the Loading Plant assets the following year, marking the end of the munition's era.

The war's aftermath took a toll on former staffers. The extreme reaction of Abram C. Cram, a Bethlehem Loading Plant chemist, drew an unwelcome spotlight to the personal adversities many encountered. Thrown into abrupt unemployment, "he stepped before the fast-moving 11 o'clock express from Philadelphia."

Nor was this an issue in the ordnance business alone. Many other industries also faced oversupply and workforce disruptions as the nation transitioned to peacetime.

World War I arms industry profiteers dodged any accountability. Public unrest finally reached a tipping point in the mid-1930s. The U.S. Senate in response established the "Special Committee on Investigation of the Munitions Industry" to examine price gouging.

The task force's report pointed out that Bethlehem Loading, only one example of several, earned an eye-watering 362 percent profit in 1918 alone. President Franklin Delano Roosevelt organized a special board to draft laws for "profitless" and efficient mobilization of resources in time of war but did nothing further.

Bethlehem Loading Plant's dramatic rise and fall draws attention to the complex interplay between industry and the ethical dimensions of providing for a wartime economy. *photo loading plant interior courtesy of Atlantic County, NJ; loading plant aerial map: Hagley Museum and Library; Frances Sheridan Haut photo courtesy New Castle History and Archaeology Program*

Page 18 Suffragettes

By the time thirty-five states had ratified, Delaware's deliberations commanded the national spotlight. The stakes were high. Their "yes" vote would permanently embed the right into the Constitution. A "no" vote would plunge the suffragist drive into serious uncertainty.

The remaining six states, including Louisiana, Florida, North Carolina, Tennessee, Vermont, and Connecticut, had unpredictable stances, making Delaware's position seminal. Massachusetts, New Jersey, Pennsylvania, and Delaware had active anti-suffragist movements, further clouding the outcome. The nation watched with bated breath.

The Wilmington-based Delaware Equal Suffrage Association opened new headquarters in Dover the minute Congress passed the 19th amendment. Their president, Mabel Ridgely, saw a fight coming and wanted to be close to the action.

The First State's Democratic leaders supported early ratification. They urged fellow members in January 1920 to vote in favor if Republican governor John Townsend called a special session. But Townsend wavered, citing costs.

Mrs. Ridgely reacted, stating that her association was willing to pay the expense, given the session's importance for ratification. "The Governor replied that this was not in accord with his idea of justice," explained Mrs. Ridgely. The governor insisted that the session expense would not deter him from calling the legislature together, she noted, if he believed the action served the state's interest.

"Should he change his mind at any time," continued Mrs. Ridgely, "our offer to finance the session holds good. With twenty-six active auxiliaries in the state, we would have no difficulty in raising sufficient funds. The women of Delaware are very decidedly in earnest in this matter of their political freedom."

Mrs. Ridgely emphasized the inevitability of National Woman Suffrage in a February 14 letter to the *Evening Journal*. She compared any attempt to halt the movement to trying to sweep back the tide with a broom.

Mary Wonderly Scott, vice-president of the Delaware Anti-Suffrage Association, responded the following week with her group's view of the matter. "We are perfectly willing to submit the amendment to a vote of the people and abide by their decision. That is the decision that has been reached in other states where the amendment has not been ratified and is one of the fairest tests to settle the question."

On March 6, 1920, Governor Townsend called for a special session. "As to the woman's suffrage proposition," commented the *Evening Journal*, "it is now clearly up to the General Assembly. The Governor has passed the question up to the legislators. The members who have been smilingly pussy footing will now have to stand up and be counted." Dover commanded national attention for several weeks. Newspapers from across the country reported the ups and downs of the state's struggle.

Governor Townsend acknowledged the honest opposition but emphasized that Delaware could not afford to delay women the right to vote. "The time has come that makes it imperative for us to grant the right (and it is right) to those who do wish to play a part," he said.

The *Baltimore Sun*'s editorial page weighed in on March 12. "Our deduction is that the suffrage amendment will be ratified by Delaware's Legislature. But still, we find a feeling of uncertainty. Some members of the Legislature, heretofore hostile to suffrage, have lined up for it. Still, we could not find that assurance had been given by the necessary majority."

Snapped Mrs. Scott, "If the cohorts of suffrage carry their banners to victory through the Delaware Legislature it will only be after they have fought their way through the ranks of the anti's."

Delaware suffragist efforts stalled at the special session's June 2 vote. "SUFFRAGE DEAD" declared the *Evening Journal*'s June 3rd, page 1 headline. "Anti-suffragists in the House made good on a threat yesterday afternoon and allowed the ratification resolution to die in the House committee," said the lede. "Friends of suffrage made an attempt to have the resolution considered in committee but failed." The Legislature adjourned *sine die* ("without a day"), indicating a recess of the legislative session short of specifying a reconvening date.

Delaware, the first state to ratify the Constitution, failed when called upon to do likewise with the 19th amendment. The 36th state vote would have to be found elsewhere. *'By Gum!' postcard courtesy Ken Florey Suffrage Collection/Gado Images; suffragists on train platform: from the collection of Paul Preston Davis; suffragist at blackboard cartoon courtesy Ann Lewis Women's Suffrage Collection*

Page 19 Delaware State Fair

An 1897 advertisement presented the festival as a "clean, vigorous, dignified, and comprehensive exposition." The Pennsylvania Railroad had special excursions, departing from various depots in Maryland and across Delaware. However, the good times were about to stop.

Looming public concerns of tuberculosis overshadowed the 1900 fair. This led the state to withhold annual funding indefinitely. The Dover Golf Club took advantage of the pause, purchased the Fairview Park grounds, and built a course there.

Delaware's public had no state fair to attend for the next decade. "Ten years ago, when a State Fair on its last leg begged the Legislature for a saving pittance, the aristocrats fought it off," stated a disgusted 1907 letter to the editor of the *Evening Journal*. "Since that time the State has exhibited discreditably at one fair in another State, and now at another, and spent more money on them than a home fair would have cost her," hissed the writer.

During the years without a state fair, Wilmington's Brandywine Springs Agricultural Fair held a dependable alternative. The group reincorporated as Delaware State Fair Association, Inc. (DSFA) and revived the Delaware State Fair name. They relocated the fairgrounds in 1910 to the city's Wawaset Park in search of a wider audience.

Six years later, in 1916, the DSFA learned that the DuPont Company planned to buy Wawaset Park, intending to develop the land into a residential community. Anticipating possible fair disruption, the DSFA in early 1917 promptly acquired a new land parcel. This replacement, in the adjacent town of Elsmere, introduced a new fairground that included a racetrack for horses, cars, and motorcycles. That September, the new grounds hosted the fair, which drew a record crowd, with a single-day head count of 25,000 people.

Residents of Kent and Sussex counties, meanwhile, felt the need for their own fair. In 1919, a group of Harrington harness racing businessmen formulated plans. The next January, they incorporated the Kent and Sussex County Fair Association, Inc. (KSCFA).

The KSCFA acquired a 30-acre plot in Harrington, financed by a bond issue of 1,200 shares at $25 each. They sought to revive the fair's rural roots. A diverse crowd attended the inaugural fair from July 27-30, 1920. Admission prices: 25¢ for children and 50¢ for adults.

The two fairs each thrived for several years. The DSFA existed until 1928 with the September Elsmere event. Then, the Delaware State Fair Association, Inc. relocated to Harrington, merging with Kent and Sussex County Fair. The combined organization marked the genesis of today's Delaware State Fair. *Man with Sheep-Hagley Museum and Library; Postcard-Delaware Public Archive/Caley Postcards*

Page 20 Mulholland Spoons

Financial record discrepancies soon arose, piquing owner John Mulholland's suspicion and threatening to expose Welch's covert operations. The founder discovered Welch's unauthorized withdrawal of $35,000 and implemented tighter oversight of company books.

Black, for his part, continued to trust Welch, not aware of these new constraints. Welch approached him for a $25,000 loan, collateralized by a Mulholland Company note, to purchase stock and clear debts.

Welch's dubious conduct continued unabated. He subsequently initiated a series of events that threatened the business's very viability. The schemer found a loophole in the new accounting rules in July 1953 and brazenly withdrew an additional $9,500.

In August, Welch's behavior began to break down as his dealings with Howard Black took a darker turn. Black and Welch met ostensibly to discuss payback of the $25,000 loan. Welch instead deflected the issue by fast talking his counterpart into buying stock in a new com pany he was setting up. He squeezed Black for an additional $8,000 loan.

Welch in September obtained a $150,000 loan from Farmers Bank in Delaware, collateralized by his pyramid scheme. He utilized these monies to acquire the remaining company stock, all while altering the corporation's name.

Welch's control of his new company—Welch Manufacturing— seemed secure until his sudden disappearance on October 30, 1953, triggering a police search across 13 states.

Black, fearing a big loss, went to court on November 16 to seek a judgment for the monies. The court ruled in his favor. Moreover, Farmers Bank had by then recalled the $150,000 loan after John Mulholland tipped them off to the internal company thefts. As a result, they held a sheriff's sale on November 20 at which the bank bought out Welch Manufacturing.

Welch's whereabouts remained a mystery until November 23. A maid in NYC's Bretton Hall Hotel found a note reading: "Don't go into the bathroom—suicide. Call police." She ran screaming into the hall and attracted a nearby bellboy. Rescuers managed to save Welch.

Welch's corporate legacy in tatters, his reputation ruined, he stumbled along, trying to keep his life together. He incorporated a new Milford company in December 1954, Mulco Products, Inc., focusing on...wooden spoons!

Howard Black by 1956 still awaited the court-mandated payment from Welch. Challenging the ruling, Welch filed a petition with the Chancery Court to void his judgment.

A surprising turn led to a judge concluding that Welch had the authority to borrow the $25,000 from Black on behalf of Mulholland Company. "The transaction was never consummated in that Welch became ill," Judge Charles L. Terry alluded to Welch's hotel incident. "The pledgee of his shares foreclosed its loan, thus divesting Welch completely of any interest whatsoever in the corporation."

The court thereby upheld Welch's petition to have the $25,000 judgment invalidated. The ruling handed Welch a lifeline, enabling him to sidestep the financial consequences of his actions. Howard Black, on the other hand, got stuck with the tab.

Clarence Welch in September 1957 sold his home in trust to his lawyer, perhaps fearing further legal ramifications. Meanwhile, Mulco continued to produce wooden spoons, but the mid-twentieth century had brought the advent of plastic. Lacking the charm of gumwood but certainly cheaper to manufacture.

Sensing a permanent shift in the market, Welch cut his involvement with Mulco and wooden products altogether in 1963. He went on to found Mohawk Electrical Systems, where he applied both life and business lessons learned.

Welch successfully led Mohawk as CEO until his death in 1998 at the age of 85. Notably absent from Clarence M. Welch's obituary were any mentions of Welch Manufacturing or Mulco Products, Inc., a quiet acknowledgment of a chapter best left in the dustbin. *Mulholland spoon package: public domain; photo of early Mulholland plant courtesy Milford Museum*

Page 21 First Study Abroad

His fervor caught the attention of the French government, culminating in his receipt of the 1925 "Officier d'Academie" award. This international recognition attests to the academic merits and underscores the exchange's role in fortifying Franco-American ties. The course's inclusivity grew exponentially. The department opened the program to women and other universities.

British Rhodes scholar G. Billy Carter, visiting the Parisian study enclave, was astounded by the electric atmosphere. The students were not just transient academic tourists, he observed, but committed to exploiting a unique learning platform.

Notable French academics sang praises for the undertaking. Professor Charles Cestre from the Sorbonne, in correspondence with Dr. Hullihen, extolled the students' academic achievements. He marveled at their personal growth. This commendation added a layer of scholarly legitimacy to the Delaware Foreign Study Plan, so that future studies abroad became a template.

Kirkbride's untimely demise in 1929, at age 36, dealt a devastating blow. However, by then, his endeavor in global educational pursuits had attracted 44 students from 28 colleges. Though he could not witness the long-term effect of his vision, his impact proved indomitable. Academic powerhouses like Princeton and Harvard lost no time replicating his model.

Today, the University of Delaware perpetuates the professor's memory through scholarships and a Parisian library established in his name. The French government awarded him the "Officier de l'Instruction Publique" and the "Chevalier de la Legion d'Honneur."

Raymond Watson Kirkbride's legacy reinforces the enduring relevance of global outreach. His innovative venture has become an integral part of the American educational ecosystem, one that will influence higher education for generations to come. *All photos this page University of Delaware Archives*

Page 22 Broiler Industry

Confronted with the challenge of caring for this huge, unexpected surplus of yellow chicks, she chose to keep the bounty. This allowed her to earn additional income by selling the surplus as broilers. Steele promptly got busy and made way for additional housing.

The sudden influx of birds posed a real problem, as Steele now had more chickens than she could let freely roam. Confronted with this head-spinning situation, she embarked on an innovative experiment. Steele decided to raise all 500 chicks in confinement.

The move must have seemed counterintuitive to the average person: didn't chickens require ample outdoor space? Weren't fresh air and sunlight essential for their wellbeing? Son David pointed out later the concept of raising chickens solely indoors was a brand-new idea.

Steele had only paid for 50; if most did not survive, that was her gamble. Sixteen weeks in, Cecile Steele had an "Aha!" moment. Despite initial doubts, most chicks survived to a marketable weight of 2-¼ pounds, earning Steele 62 cents per pound. Cecile was so pleased with her results that she started with 1,000 birds the following year—all to be sold as broilers and every one of them housed indoors.

The broiler-only approach seemed risky in the early 1920s when chickens were expensive. The purchase of a single bird required four hours of work. Onlookers questioned if a large enough audience existed to justify commercializing broilers over egg production.

The Roaring '20s dawned as a period of immense growth, providing Americans with more disposable income. A societal shift in outlook, coupled with advancements in agricultural technology, supported Cecile Steele's entry into the broiler business. Additionally, the establishment of grocery store chains, from small towns to big cities, also played a vital role in boosting her business. Consequently, chicken dinners, once regarded as a special occasion meal, evolved into a commonplace every-day staple on tables across the nation.

Steele's husband, David Wilmer Steele, soon quit his job as a Coast Guard captain to join her booming business.

Delmarva's mild climate, abundant lumber, and proximity by truck/train/ship to big city markets made the region an ideal location for this fledgling industry.

Managing large poultry sheds presented new challenges, including waste disposal and disease control. The Steeles continued to innovate, while overlooking day-to-day distractions, even shifting from standalone poultry sheds to connected structures.

The Steele's success indeed inspired awe throughout the peninsula. Their less prosperous Delmarva neighbors, observing this pioneering accomplishment, began to take notice. Driven by a desperate need for profitable ventures, others quickly aligned themselves with Cecile Steele's strategies. A contemporary journalist estimated that Baltimore Hundred alone raised 50,000 broilers in 1925. This expansion of the local economy soon spurred Delaware to proudly claim the title of 'Broiler Capital of the World.' The Steele operations had soared by 1926 to about 10,000 chickens a year.

Around 1934, David Steele formed the Indian River Poultry Hatchery in Ocean View with partner George Keen. David ventured beyond their business in 1937, winning an election to the state Senate.

David and Cecile's success ended tragically when the couple died in a 1940 yacht explosion. Despite their untimely death, the Steeles left behind an enduring impact. Their large-scale broiler model continues to fuel the American poultry industry.

The Delaware Women's Hall of Fame in 1983 honored Cecile Long Steele's groundbreaking contributions by inducting her into their esteemed ranks. *watercolor by Theresa (Terre) Walton, for the Delaware Women's Hall of Fame; interior photo of chicken house Delaware Agricultural Museum collection*

Page 23 Baseball Hall of Famer

The Red Sox reported to San Antonio, Texas spring training in March 1924. "Charles Ruffing, big blond hurler, drew favorable comments ... because of his fastball and curve," stated an Associated Press item. Ruffing's teammates promptly tagged him with the nickname "Red" thanks to his hair color. His wife, however, always called him Charles.

Rookie Ruffing played 8 games in Boston in the first 3 months of the 1924 season. Team secretary James Price announced on July 25 that the Sox had sent Ruffing to the Dover Senators. "We can recall him on 48-hours' notice," Price quickly added.

Ruffing pitched his first Dover game the following day and "halted the losing streak of the Eastern Shore League leaders. The former Red Soxer defeated the Parksley Spuds, 6-3, and helped win his own game with a home run drive," reported the *Wilmington News-Journal*.

During his time in Dover, Ruffing lasted 94 innings over 15 games, with a lackluster 4-7 record. Nevertheless, the Red Sox recalled him,

86

glimpsing something about his pitching style. He never returned to the minors. Ruffing nevertheless struggled with the Red Sox through five mediocre seasons. The team finally traded him to the New York Yankees in 1930.

Charles "Red" Ruffing went on to pitch in seven World Series with the Yanks: 1932, 1936-39, and 1941-42. He is considered one of the most successful postseason pitchers in baseball history, boasting a World Series record of 7 wins and 2 losses.

Decades later, in the twilight of a stellar career, Ruffing received a 1967 phone call from the *News Journal* sports editor. Al Cartwright congratulated him on his Hall of Fame induction and asked Ruffing about his most vivid Delaware memory.

"Peaches," he responded. "We hopped around the league on buses, and I can still see us stopping along a road to help ourselves whenever we came to an orchard. That used to break up the monotony of the trips — the peaches, and riding on top of the bus."

Page 24 Citizen's Police Reserves

Lack of adequate training resulted in excessive or inappropriate use of authority, mishandling of situations, and potential life endangerment. The CHPRC was infiltrated by opportunists, often treating their positions as rewards for political favors. Cronyism resulted in a force ripe for confusion and inefficiency.

Appointee William B. Foster, a high-ranking DuPont official, misused his authority, violating speeding laws at will. Asa Bennett served as a Republican state senator from 1920-22, while simultaneously being a CHPRC member. He issued more speeding tickets in 1921 than any of the other associated officers. His political enemies took to the roads at their own peril.

The group's governing body, the State Highway Commission, acknowledged T. Coleman du Pont's robust contribution to the financing of Route 13. They appointed his son Frank to the CHPRC as a token of recognition. The younger du Pont transitioned directly from the volunteer force to the overseeing agency. Shortly thereafter, he became chairman, remaining with the Commission from 1922-1949.

Another example of the CHPRC's dynamics emerged with Julia Hays Tallwoman. Her exceptional Republican fundraising efforts were rewarded with membership in the CHPRC. She went on to become the national committeewoman for Delaware's Republican Party.

Similarly, Clement B. Hallam, a prominent editor at *The Evening Journal* and a staunch Republican Party supporter, received a CHPRC badge. This gesture from the State Highway Commission tacitly acknowledged his standing and contributions.

Counterproductive political appointments undermined CHPRC's legitimacy. The public perceived the force as being more focused on maintaining loyalty than on law enforcement. CHPRC observers howled over the compromised impartiality within two years of the division's formation. "This shows the fallacy," cried a *Newark Ledger* editorial, "of having such a citizens' corps of men to carry out the law. It's nothing short of lunacy to turn men loose to enforce the law when they will abuse the law for their own indulgence.

"Such half-baked officers are a danger," the editorial thundered. "They act as spies and with a badge pinned under a coat lapel, they sneak up and cause trouble for the motorist who may exceed his 30 miles an hour by a trifle on a straight stretch of open highway."

The decisive creation of the Delaware State Police in 1925 rectified the discord and inadequacies of the Citizens' Highway Police Reserve Corps. The reorganization acknowledged the necessity of a well-structured paid constabulary. Law enforcement relies heavily on community trust and cooperation. Delaware, thus, laid a strong foundation for fair policing that can adapt to public safety needs.

Page 25 Rum-runners

The coastal patrol encountered other issues, including limits on overall enforcement. U.S. policing extended out to only three nautical miles. Lack of training and experience posed a material challenge for the maritime security services, nor were tactics and procedures in place for criminal law encounters.

From 1920 to the end of Prohibition, given an expanded budget, the Coast Guard transformed itself. The updated task force evolved into an intimidating presence for Delaware Bay rum-runners. The Guard strategically deployed cutter ships and aircraft to amplify growing regulatory capabilities. They added aviation units for surveillance and reconnaissance, plus established additional air stations. This expansion included procuring seaplanes and aircraft like the Curtiss HS-2L flying boats, to intercept moonshiners.

The Coast Guard commissioned new vessel construction, tailoring designs expressly for Prohibition enforcement. Additionally, they adapted existing ships to this new mandate, including 20 surplus Navy destroyers. The expanded fleet empowered the coastline patrol to combat smuggling on a broader scale. Furthermore, the Navy and Customs Service synchronized federal law enforcement efforts.

Illegal bay alcohol operations attracted suppliers from all points of the compass. Canadian whisky schooners targeted the Philadelphia and New Jersey markets. Bahamian smugglers regularly used 'bank boats' (shallow draft skiffs) to land their Scotch whisky in the dunes between Bethany and Rehoboth.

Rum-runners employed recently invented hydroplanes to transport packaged "case goods" from incoming ocean steamships. Such ships anchored in the mid-bay area, referred to as 'rum row,' where they fell beyond the reach of the law. The emboldened rum-runners believed their newly acquired speed would provide a substantial edge over the Coast Guard. *The Helena,* for example, combined this speed with cargo capacity. She boasted deep, spacious hatches, a draft of merely 3.5 feet, and a 45-foot length, navigating easily while laden with contraband.

The Coast Guard saw pressing need to assert authority on the open waters. Rum-runners outpacing them was unacceptable and posed a threat to the Guard's dominion. Focusing their efforts on this prized catch, the police sought to make an example of *The Helena.*

Reedy Island, several miles south of Fort Delaware and just offshore of Port Penn, sometimes posed perilous situations. During adverse weather, Guard patrols often came across a partially concealed jetty linking Reedy Island to the shore. Such invisible hazards caused serious risks, leading to accidents. The fog of January 1930 exemplified this danger, with the sinking of Cutter No. 211.

Criminal syndicates employed "pay-off men" to engage in bribery. However, the Guard stood firm. "The Coast Guard cannot be bought," asserted Commander Edward S. Addison, the commandant of section base No. 9 in Cape May, NJ. He shared instances where one patrol boatswain was offered $5,000 "just to ease up a little" and another $10,000 to "close his eyes for a while."

There were law officials who did not resist. For example, pay-off man John "Chick" Callahan testified about traveling from northern New Jersey to Cumberland County "to make arrangements with the sheriff down there." During his 1950 trial he recalled his involvement with Joseph H. Reinfeld's cartel. The mob, said Callahan, was compelled to set up a 'fix' to unload bootleg liquor along South Jersey's bay coast. The arrangement circumvented a blockade on the North Jersey shoreline.

Did the end of Prohibition eliminate rum-running in Delaware Bay? No! "Speedboats loaded with fine imported wines are not seized daily as they used to be," The *News Journal* reported in 1935, "but alcohol smuggling continues a thriving business for syndicates which now try to cheat the government of taxes."

Prohibition sought to curtail societal ills. However, this measure inadvertently fostered other forms of misconduct. Rum-runners provided fertile ground for the escalation of official corruption, graft, and racketeering. *Rum-runner photo National Archives ID 205590832*

Page 26 Sweet Potatoes

A duo of cultural changes exponentially propelled the national sweet potato market.

First, radio's new advertising techniques boosted demand in broader regional markets. Second, the development of integrated trucking and rail delivery networks provided farmers with the means to swiftly deliver produce at times of peak demand.

Farmers dug their sweet potatoes in early October. The bounty needed sufficient time curing in a farm based 'potato house' to improve flavor and nutrition. Meanwhile, supply and demand rendered sweet potato marketing seasonal—highly sought after for Thanksgiving and Christmas but not much before. Growers, in the interim, held each annual harvest in the potato house, which post-curing doubled as storage.

Come holiday time, brokers purchased the sweets and transferred them to large wholesale facilities. Railways in Laurel or Seaford, or barges on the adjacent Nanticoke River, conducted the final shipping.

Many of the farmers worked closely with Vic Moore of Seaford, Harvey Hastings of Laurel, and Seaford's J. A. Morgan, the era's largest year-round produce broker. The latter, with ready access to Philadelphia and New York markets, considered sweet potatoes his number one money-maker.

Seaford's mayor, John Eskridge, built Delmarva's largest sweet potato storage house in 1921, with a 100,000 half-bushel basket capacity. Johnson & Company's 1927 facility dwarfed Eskridge's plant, boasting a 250,000-basket capacity. Seaford's surrounding countryside produced approximately 250,000 baskets by 1935. The town emerged as the commercial storage regional center. Up to 1,200 sweet potato-filled railroad cars annually left neighboring Laurel.

The ascent of the bright orange vegetable, fueled by other technological advances, continued through a pre-World War II boom. The peninsula's limited tillable acreage eventually meant Delaware farmers could no longer compete with other states. Post war, the First State's sweet potato industry lost national standing as other states expanded. *Johnson Potato Storage House in Seaford & potato house interior courtesy Delaware Public Archives/Delaware Board of Agriculture Collection, Phillips Potato House photo LR Wall/Wikipedia*

Page 27 Indian River Bay

Their catch was worth that inconvenience: the same rapid tidal action likewise oxygenated the local shellfish beds and enabled them to flourish. Thus, a booming seafood industry arose around the bay's perimeter. Good fishing grounds and specialized navigation requirements drove a constant demand for small trading shallops and flat-bottomed coastal schooners. This led to the growth of numerous mom-and-pop shipyards along the Indian River and a host of surrounding tributaries.

Late nineteenth century canal digging in nearby Lewes, Rehoboth, and Assawoman Bay consistently disrupted the current. These new Indian River Bay Inlet channels, along with unending coastal storms, contributed to gradual silting.

Shell fishing suffered from the diminished flow. Moreover, this decrease led to a decline in the once abundant annual spawning runs of herring and shad in nearby rivers and creeks. Local watermen shoveled valiantly to maintain open channels, to no avail. By 1920, the Indian River Inlet had sealed itself shut, marking an end to navigability.

"The water had become more or less stagnated," reported the *Morning News* on November 5, 1928, "killing the fish there and destroying a fish industry that for years was profitable to residents of the Indian River section. Efforts to get adequate federal aid had been unavailing. The state appropriated some money for that purpose, but it was not sufficient to provide a permanent inlet." Public pressure to restore the inlet built throughout the 1920s. The first official recovery effort met with a spectacular lack of success.

Senator John G. Townsend, Jr. and several other prominent citizens proposed to use 2 tons of dynamite to accomplish the refurbishment. Spectators from nearby towns, villages, and farms flocked to the inlet by foot, horseback, boat, or in Durban wagons to witness the spectacle. Young James C. Townsend tagged along with his Uncle John to watch. "When they exploded it, the sand went up in the air and came right back down," he recalled with a smile years later. "Sand's unpredictable, you know."

Diesel-powered dredging technology finally provided the breakthrough that engineers at Indian River Bay Inlet needed to combat ongoing silt accumulation. In late summer 1938, the *Margate*, a large hydraulic dredge ship, arrived with the power to shift considerable sand volumes. Delaware contracted Hill Dredging Co. to create a 15-foot deep, 200-foot-wide waterway. The *Margate*'s design centered around a suction pipe, or dredge ladder, equipped with a motor-powered cutting head to agitate and loosen sediment. A centrifugal pump created a vacuum to draw the sediment-water mixture through the suction pipe, with the pump's efficiency dependent on factors like flow rate and abrasion resistance. The dredged material was then transported through a discharge line, while the dredge's hull housed essential machinery, ensuring stability, buoyancy, and efficient operation.

The *Margate*, and subsequent models, effectively resolved the silting issue, resulting in a coastal engineering marvel. Traditional bucket and shovel methods became obsolete, as did the novel idea of dynamite silt removal. *Inlet photo: Delaware State Parks collection*

Page 28 Oystermen

Spawning makes them softer and less flavorful, which isn't what you want on your plate. Besides, in these warmer months, the risk of bacteria associated with foodborne illnesses is higher. Oysters feed by filtering water, which can concentrate toxic algae, potentially making them unsafe to eat. The "R" rule is not as critical today thanks to modern refrigeration and aquaculture practices that ensure oysters can be safely consumed year-round.

Rudimentary forces emerged in 1868 for oyster bed self-policing to prevent competitive poaching. The watermen identified and guarded the coveted locations of the most fruitful oyster beds, drawing on generations of hand-me-down experience. They used guns to defend their turf.

The treasured Eastern oyster *(Crassostrea virginica)* carried special weight for the Kent County towns of Little Creek, Bowers Beach, Leipsic, and Port Mahon. This epicenter of the Delaware oyster industry had, by 1885, doubled annual production to 20 million bushels.

Oyster watermen—'oyster tongers'—used long, rake-like tools to gather oysters from the bottom of the bay and surrounding estuaries. Hand tongs are long, scissor-like tools with metal rakes on the ends. The implements are very long, heavy, and difficult to manage. Thus, hand tonging is hard, slow work.

The waterman, standing on the side of his boat, would open the tongs and reach down to the seafloor. The bottom might be fifteen feet deep or more. He closed the tongs, scooping oysters between both rakes. Sometimes each "lick" of the tongs brought up only a few oysters. The tonger then swiveled toward the deck and dumped the oysters onto the "culling board," where the crew sorted their catch.

Reefs regularly produce attached clusters of large and small oysters. The waterman used a "culling hammer" to separate the two. The device's handle also had a measuring gauge. Any oyster smaller than three inches had to be returned to the bed. The rise of nineteenth-century dredging technology, coupled with the growth of oyster farming, led to the occupational disappearance of the oyster tonger. The *Maggie S. Myers,* built in 1893 and still in service, is the oldest of the oyster schooners working out of Leipsic and Little Creek. The two-masted schooner is typical of late nineteenth and early twentieth century oystering ships.

These crafts, with their shallow drafts, were perfectly suited to the bay's limited depths, enabling seamless navigation. Moreover, their design allowed them to accumulate substantial oyster quantities, optimizing economic efficiency.

Oystermen devoted their days to dredging or tonging and offloaded their catch onto a "buy boat" — a floating intermediary that saved them time-consuming shore trips. These middlemen linked the harvesters with the wholesale and retail marketers. The buy boats typically had ice and other supplies to preserve oyster freshness. Their captains, upon collecting from multiple harvesters, headed inland. This system was beneficial for all parties involved: oystermen could maximize their time and effort on the water, and markets could receive large quantities of oysters quickly, ensuring the consumer a fresh product.

Annual Delaware oyster 'landings' throughout the early 1900s ranged from one million to two million bushels (typically weighing 45-60 pounds per bushel). The trade employed 7,000 men in 1933. The MSX (Multinucleated Sphere Unknown) parasite dramatically reduced oyster production by the 1950s. The outbreak inflicted serious ecological and economic damage. Many oyster beds were nearly wiped out, along with the livelihoods of the people who depended on oyster harvesting.

Harvesters collected in 1960 a mere 49,000 bushels from the bay. Delaware oysterman employment numbers had plummeted by 1967. The MSX outbreak highlighted the urgent need to step up the bay's ecological monitoring. *Oyster tongs: collection Bowers Beach Maritime Museum; oyster schooners by Marion Warren/Maryland State Archives*

Page 29 Civilian Conservation Corps

Young men between the ages of 18 and 25, unmarried, unemployed, and U.S. citizens, could enlist in the program. The CCC provided an essential economic boost at a time when money was scarce. Enrollees received $30 a month and sent most of that pay home to their families. This injection pumped an estimated $5,000 a month into Delaware's economy, providing much-needed community relief.

One recruit was soon-to-be-famous artist Jack Lewis. This Baltimore native joined the Delaware CCC in 1936. His assignments included sketching the daily activities at four locations. These Lewes, Magnolia, Slaughter Beach and Leipsic marshland camps focused on drainage ditch mosquito control.

Jack Lewis found his footing in the CCC, fell in love with Delaware, and later moved there permanently. Lewis went on to become a man of many accomplishments. He was honored with the Governor's Award of Arts in 1981 and received the highest civilian honor for meritorious service, the Order of the First State, in 2010. He died at age 99 in York, ME, where he had moved in 1998.

Bombay Hook National Wildlife Refuge, due east of Smyrna, is a living monument to the CCC's efforts. Spanning roughly 16,000 coastal acres, this sanctuary comprises a vast and varied natural habitat. Civilian Conservation Corps members based at Leipsic constructed dikes, buildings, water control structures, and impoundments. The CCC built Raymond Pool, removed timber from Shearness and Finis swamps, built a 99-foot lookout tower, ran ditches for mosquito control, and conducted various wildlife surveys.

Delawareans' quality of life rapidly improved, thanks to the CCC. In just one year, from 1936 to 1937, the Corps constructed vehicle bridges, laid sewer lines, and executed widespread mosquito control measures. World War II's demands for physically fit men took precedence over the Civilian Conservation Corps. The CCC formally closed their doors on June 30, 1942. Congress redirected the program funds to support the war effort. The CCC's endeavors produced a lasting heritage in Delaware and across the United States. The program imparted to its men a renewed sense of dignity and future direction. *Jack Lewis watercolor courtesy Delaware Division of Historical and Cultural Affairs*

Page 30 American Liberty League

This new group named itself the American Liberty League, designed to vehemently oppose the 1935 Social Security Act. The backers saw the New Deal as a perilous slide towards socialism, bankruptcy, and dictatorship. The League's stated purpose was to "defend and uphold the Constitution" and "foster the right to work, earn, save, and acquire property."

One name stood out among the ranks of the movement's founders: Irénée du Pont, whose money largely bankrolled the group. The former DuPont president ardently backed the crusaders, championing laissez-faire economics. "The federal government's present methods of doling out other people's money for relief are in direct violation of the Constitution," du Pont charged. He made this assertion in an October interview, at a time when public debate raged over the role of government in economic recovery.

Along with his peers, staunch private industry and Constitutional government advocates, he deemed the Social Security Act overreach. The League held that such programs should remain within the purview of the states. Furthermore, the coalition argued against mandatory employer contributions.

These captains of industry believed this funding would lay an excessive burden on businesses. Social Security would impede economic growth and infringe upon the principles of individual liberty. Foremost, they saw FDR's visions as free enterprise intrusions. They advo cated a voluntary system or "alternative approaches" for the era's economic upheaval. Their opposition extended beyond Social Security. For example, they saw the Agricultural Adjustment Administration as representative: "a vicious combination of Fascism, Socialism, and Communism which cannot be harmonized with the basic principles of Constitutional government in the United States."

The organization's literature brimmed with a distinctive purple prose: "Work relief: a record of the tragic failure of the most costly governmental experiment in world history." The American Liberty League membership grew within two years to 25,000. Both the U.S. Chamber of Commerce and the National Association of Manufacturers supported them. Despite these advantages, their message failed to reach a broad audience. The organization's backing of Republican presidential candidate Alfred Landon hardly made an impact.

Roosevelt rode back into office in a 1936 landslide victory. Only Maine and Vermont embraced Landon. The public had resoundingly affirmed FDR's New Deal. Du Pont's group quietly retreated following this decisive defeat. They folded entirely in 1940.

The American Liberty League did leave one legacy. The group's framework and ideology paved the way for an ensuing trend of Constitutional nationalism. This wave, although not organizationally linked, included movements such as the 1950s John Birch Society and, five decades later, the Tea Party, both of which echoed similar principles. American Liberty League's successors—rejecting all else as dangerously foreign—likewise aimed for a re-dedication to the nation's true Constitutional values. *Liberty League lawyers photo: Library of Congress; Liberty League logo public domain; Daniel Fitzpatrick cartoon for St. Louis Post-Dispatch: Library of Congress*

Page 31 Rural Electrification

Cooke extended an invitation to private power systems to join hands with REA's program. The proposal was that utilities should contribute 40 to 50 cents for every government dollar invested to broaden the reach of power lines. Private firms could shoulder 95% of the government's program responsibilities. Cooke assured established providers that financing terms would be adaptable. His insistence played a crucial role in ensuring the program would eventually become self-sustaining. Furthermore, the REA underlined the necessity to at least cover costs. If utilities chose not to participate, warned Cooke, REA would seize the reins and assume the authority to generate, transmit, and distribute power.

Private utilities in response proposed a $238 billion version of the program, with the condition that the government supply most of the funds. They shook hands and made a deal.

Delaware's local REA affiliate got underway in 1936, stringing 94 miles of wire to reach 223 Kent and Sussex County customers. "Modern electric lights gleamed from the windows of 31 farmhouses west and northwest of Greenwood for the first time last night," reported the *Morning News* on March 24, 1938. "'There she is!' farmers exclaimed as bulbs began to glow. Dobbin neighed and Rover barked. After that families had a merry time getting used to the switches, hooking up new gadgets, and telling each other what difference it made."

Lee C. Prickett, agricultural engineer for the REA, addressed a mass meeting of farmers in Georgetown early in 1938. "With electric power on the farm," he said, "the water pump and the electric washer become two of the family's most important implements." Headquartered at Greenwood's old Queen Anne Railroad station, the project made great strides over two years. A one-million-dollar investment led to 800 miles of crisscrossing electric wires, providing neighborhood service to the state's lower two counties. The REA hosted a Delaware traveling educational caravan in May. This first roadshow aimed to educate farmers on creative electrical uses. Delighted onlookers marveled at quirky displays, including a sculpted cow that produced milk via powered milking machines.

From the project's 1935 launch to the spring of 1940, electricity reached approximately 17% of Delaware's 11,000 farms. REA anticipated that by fall, 35% of the state's farms would have access. Indeed, by autumn more than a third owned electric refrigerators. A considerable portion had vacuum cleaners, and a vast majority possessed radios. Farmers milked Bessie while she moo-ved to the radio's beat!

War Production Board Director Donald M. Nelson halted REA's copper allocations only months after the December 1941 attack on Pearl Harbor. This strategic war measure aimed to conserve resources throughout World War II. As a result, any new electric buildout halted until the war concluded in 1945.

Delaware's REA reorganized into the Delaware Electric Cooperative Inc. (DEC) in 1946. This new entity delivered power to more than 54,000 rural customers by 1947 and maintained 4,500 miles of wire. Cooperatives and private utilities by 1948 had brought electricity to 75% of First State farmers.

In the following decade Delaware's state, county, and local governments collaborated with electric co-ops and private utilities. Their 1950s efforts centered around educating and engaging the public about the best usage of electricity and a host of labor-saving devices. William E. Tarbell, for example, Kent County agricultural agent, discussed electricity at Dover's Capital Grange. His March 1951 meeting emphasized electric wiring for safety and economy. Later that same year, James R. Carroll, DEC agricultural engineer, met World War II veterans at Georgetown High School. He aimed to show how two and three wire electric circuits are constructed.

The Rural Electrification Administration's impact cannot be overstated. Ninety-seven percent of U.S. farms were electrified by 1960.

Delaware was no exception. *1942 Philco radio courtesy Greater Harrington Historical Society; iron courtesy Delaware Agricultural Museum*

Page 32 1938 Hurricane

Mid-nineteenth century meteorologists were already noticing a pattern of one hurricane about every four years. Scientists categorize hurricane wind speeds on a scale from 1 to 5. A Category 1 gale in 1903, for example, ushered in 74-95 mph wind speeds. Category 2 hurricanes, like the one that swept across the First State in 1936, are more destructive, blasting through at 96-110 mph. These rip off roofs and sidings, uproot trees, and cause power loss. The Great Hurricane of 1938 was called that for a reason. This Category 3 storm shook Delaware and went on to wallop further north. Seismographs as far away as Alaska detected the impact's intensity.

The Coast Guard and U.S. Weather Bureau closely tracked the season's first squall on September 21, 1938. The Maritime Exchange for the Delaware River and Bay likewise monitored the situation. The U.S. Weather Bureau had only started officially recognizing and issuing warnings for 'hurricane season' three years earlier. Delawareans, forewarned by diligent efforts of the Coast Guard and the U.S. Weather Bureau, were prepared when the Great Hurricane struck. Their readiness paid off as the state battened down in preparation for a pounding tempest after eight days of incessant rain. The region's maritime organizations had provided residents with a clear picture of the impending hurricane, ensuring that when landfall happened, the state was braced for a humdinger.

September 21-22 news coverage vividly details the destruction: Gales whirled at 45 miles per hour, driving ships off Lewes to seek shelter behind the refuge of the Delaware Breakwater. Consolidated Fisheries anxiously awaited news from five of their menhaden boats. These howling blasts also leveled waterlogged corn fields, felled massive trees, and washed away the remaining unpicked tomato crop. Power outages engulfed Lewes Beach and plunged the town of Claymont into afternoon darkness. Flood-prone areas braced for the worst as the Christina River at Wilmington's Third Street Bridge swelled menacingly. Several inches of water submerged Causey Avenue and Mill Street near Milford's Pennsylvania Railroad station. Downpours delivered an unusually high volume of rain. From 5 p.m. on Tuesday to 3 p.m. on Wednesday, more rain fell than the total amount recorded for the entire month of the previous September.

Prevailing westerly winds intervened, pushing the hurricane's northbound Atlantic path farther away from the coast. This fortunate pattern spared Delaware from the anticipated force. The weather changed abruptly from an escalating torrent to clear conditions within a brief span of one hour. High waters began receding as the winds shifted. The mercury dipped to a season-low of 47 degrees overnight.

The sun came up the next morning bright and clear. A sense of relief permeated the towns. Shipping activities in the bay cautiously resumed, despite still-rough seas and "house high" waves off the coast. Delawareans started evaluating the devastation. The Red Cross conducted assessments to determine what relief was necessary in ravaged areas. All told, conditions ended up manageable. The state's weary residents, and their surroundings, had withstood the deluge. The most destructive hurricane Delaware would ever witness was yet to come—the Ash Wednesday Storm of 1962.

Page 33 Federal Art Project

Jeannette Eckman, the dedicated Delaware State Director, passionately conveyed the very essence of the FAP in an April 1939 radio broadcast. She said the undertaking "has made local history by putting fresh and vigorous expression in painting and drawing into forms that the whole public can appreciate and enjoy." Furthermore, the director emphasized the educational value, stating, "Art classes have filled a long-realized need in giving to those who otherwise lack it the opportunity for healthy self-expression and the chance of widening their enjoyment of life." Under Eckman's leadership, the project catalyzed creativity and public engagement across the state.

On April 13, 1939, an exhibition of FAP work took place at Wilmington's Federal Arts Center, whose opening was graced by the presence of Governor Richard C. McMullen. This event featured the artistic accomplishments of 30 talented Delaware artists. The exhibition prominently spotlighted a collection of sketches, both black & white and color, encompassing completed as well as planned murals.

Delaware's FAP sponsored talks in Wilmington by influential artists and architects. Reah Robinson, Wilmington chapter president of the American Institute of Architects, shared his insights on May 22 at the Delaware Hardware Company. Artist Frank E. Schoonover spoke at the Boys' Club two days later. These interactions sought to bring the arts beyond the confines of museums and art galleries.

David Reyam, who headed the Delaware division of a project known as the 'Index of American Design,' aimed to produce visual records and catalog elegantly designed everyday objects. In September 1939, for example, Reyam's workers detailed the provenance of a set of gold and silver chessmen. The set, crafted by "J. Lemon" and dated 1876, once belonged to John Pierpont, J. Pierpont Morgan, Sr.'s grandfather. Reyam's artists cataloged over 400 designed objects of historic interest.

The U.S. Senate Appropriations Committee, in the summer of 1939, advanced a relief bill focused on reforming the Works Progress Administration (WPA). Representative Clifton A. Woodrum (D-VA), advocated for fiscal restraint. "Certain abuses and misuses of funds," he thundered to the press, had "crept in and grown up." The bill aimed to limit WPA project budgets, and prohibit projects solely funded by the federal government. The legislation also sought to enforce decentralization by involving state and local governments.

FAP's local Delaware magazine *Progress* reacted sharply to this bill in the June/July 1939 issue. Bankson T. Holcomb, Delaware's FAP state administrator, defended the group against "organized attempts to discredit our work." Holcomb denounced "so-called funny stories, circulated by the highly paid publicity set-ups of the reactionaries, making a burlesque of the misfortunes of the unemployed."

FDR took the high road against FAP's political opponents. "Art in America has always belonged to the people and has never been the property of an academy or a class," he said. "The great Treasury projects, through which our public buildings are being decorated, are an excellent example of the continuity of this tradition. The Federal Art Project of the Works Progress Administration is a practical relief project which also emphasizes the best tradition of the democratic spirit."

Nonetheless, the bill passed in July, notably reducing federal support for arts projects. The new law mandated that such activities only proceed with partial state or local funding. This unmitigated change battered states such as Delaware. Limited resources, plus a reluctance to invest in the arts, were already obstacles to various projects. FAP withered. "Cultural interests are essential to individual happiness but are the first to be discontinued in periods of economic stress," a disheartened Eckman sighed to the *News Journal*.

1939 emerged as a defining moment for Delaware arts, both as a historical footnote, and as a beacon of cultural identity. The multi-year efforts of the Federal Art Project have a lasting impact. These activities highlight the importance of preserving and promoting bygone histories. *Detail of poster for a Federal Art Project exhibition of the Index of American Design courtesy Library of Congress; Four samples from Index of American Design courtesy National Gallery of Art; Claymont High School mural courtesy LivingNewDeal.org*

Page 34 Fenwick Island Lighthouse

An imported Parisian prism, which a watchman manually rotated every two minutes, amplified the light from whale oil lamps. The lightkeeper eventually switched to mineral oil. An 1899 upgrade to electric lamps allowed the lighthouse to cast a detectable glow up to 15 miles out at sea. The Bureau of Lighthouses replaced the Lighthouse Board in 1910 and took management of the service for the next two decades. The United States Coast Guard (USCG) in 1931 assumed responsibility for operating the country's lighthouses. The Guard that year deemed the Fenwick Island Lighthouse unnecessary for the safe navigation of Delaware Bay and promptly sold the beacon. Charles L. Gray, a recently retired lighthouse keeper, bought the old structure. He went on to keep the light lit for another 38 years.

Then, in 1978, the Coast Guard, to the surprise of Fenwick Island residents, deactivated the lighthouse and removed its Fresnel lens. This sudden action sparked a vocal community protest. The beacon, long seen as a comforting symbol of home, had etched a place in the hearts of area folks. Paul Pepper was among the most vocal preservation advocates. His lineage was intertwined with the lighthouse's history—great-grandfather David M. Warrington was the third keeper of the light, and Pepper's grandfather, Edward G. Pepper, served as an assistant keeper. Paul and his wife Dorothy became torchbearers for the cause, rallying the community to safeguard their beloved lighthouse. "The General Services Administration agreed to turn the lighthouse over to a responsible private organization that would be willing to maintain it," recalled Pepper later. "That's when we organized Friends of Fenwick Lighthouse and told them we'd guarantee the place would be well cared for if they would turn it over to us," he said.

A wave of local commitment to preserving maritime heritage surged six years after Fenwick Island Lighthouse's deactivation. The United States Lighthouse Society was established amidst this enthusiasm. Suddenly, lighthouses were valued treasures. The "Finnix" community's efforts to save their light bore fruit. They launched a letter-writing campaign, enlisting the support of a state congressional delegation. The governor's office also showed interest in obtaining the property.

Senator Joseph R. Biden, Jr. successfully requested the Coast Guard's return of the prism. This retrieved lens was indeed the very one originally installed in 1858. Preservationist Richard B. Carter prepared the lighthouse's National Historic Register nomination, building on the township's momentum.

Paul and Dorothy Pepper, spearheading the maintenance of the lighthouse, brought their vigor and dedication to guide the efforts of the Friends of Fenwick Lighthouse. In 1981, they restored the electric light, and with it, the warmth of neighborhood nostalgia. "When it was turned over to us," said Dorothy, "the Coast Guard didn't want us to use the light because it might confuse mariners who no longer need moon and stars and lighthouses to make their way past the shoals. But I said, what's a lighthouse without a light? So, the light goes on every night, just like it always has."

The lighthouse evolved into a captivating attraction for summer tourists, drawing many enthusiasts who eagerly participated in the guided tours personally conducted by the Peppers. Today, the Fenwick Island Lighthouse is listed on the National Register of Historic Places. This shining symbol of maritime history serves both as a beacon of the past, as well as a guiding light for community-led preservation. The lamp illuminates the enduring spirit of Fenwick Islanders. As Paul Pepper reminded future generations, "The state turned it over to us. It's still owned by Delaware, but the upkeep is in our hands." *Lighthouse photo: Bill Swartwout Photography; lighthouse interior cutaway drawings: National Archives at College Park – Cartographic (RDSC)*

Page 35 First Public Airport

The farms of sleepy little Hare's Corner were needed to supply the land. Only 50 families resided there in 1941. How hard could it be to convince these patriotic yeomen to move on? Their former farmlands could help America resist the Führer's potential onslaught. Earlier in the year the U.S. Senate had granted New Castle County Levy Court authority to borrow up to $750,000 to fund a civilian airport. Now, however, Civil Aeronautics Administration officials in Washington, D.C. declared this square mile location an "essential part of the airport program of national defense." The United States Army Air Forces took control of the undertaking for the war effort, rechristened as the New Castle Army Air Base.

The Levy Court gave those 50 families only a three-month window to vacate as of early May. Suddenly, they were thrust into the daunting task of packing up all their worldly possessions and preparing to relocate. For many of them, being forced to resettle in an unfamiliar and distant location led to a lifetime of trauma. Among those most deeply impacted was John T. Hopkins, a lifelong resident and the very last farmer to sell his property to the state.

For Hopkins, Hare's Corner was more than just a piece of crossroads real estate. Hopkins' land had been cultivated by the Craig family for generations. He continued their rich history of stewardship when his turn came to till the soil. He, his wife Florence, their three children, three in-laws, and two lodgers all resided in an 11-room house. Their prosperous 135-acre farm had been part of a thriving neighborhood. Eminent domain shattered this tight-knit community. Neighbors and friends became scattered. Children were uprooted from their schools. Bethel Baptist Church, and its ancient graveyard, disappeared. The community house on Schoolhouse Lane vanished.

Aviation construction loomed. The overnight landing field encroachment upended an entire way of life. The results unfolded with alarming speed. Hopkins advertised his dilemma: his public auction ad stated he had been "compelled to discontinue farming due to the new airport development on his land." The auctioneer's gavel fell on June 16th for "anything needed for a well-equipped farm." Hopkins' notice makes clear just how much he and his family were giving up: "4 head of horses and mules, 52 head of cows and heifers, good Guernsey and Jersey, 9 with calves, manure by load or ton, baled mixed hay by the ton, redskin potatoes, 8 shoats, poultry: 75 chickens, lots of Muscovy ducks, household furniture and feather beds, two good coal heaters."

The authorities provided a "just compensation" allowance falling short of fairness. This starkly contrasted with the promised equitable treatment by the Levy Court. A "condemnation commission" awarded John and Florence Hopkins $63,400 for their farm on July 24, 1941. They immediately appealed for a case review. The family asked for $500 an acre plus $20,000 compensation for field crops, residence, farm buildings, cattle loss, and moving expenses. The commission had only budgeted $470 an acre. They made no allowances to pay for any other outstanding damages. Meanwhile, Levy Court was not about to wait for any further Hopkins case review. Instead, they orchestrated a comprehensive auction spanning the entire airport construction zone. This July 25 event included the disposal of forty-two structures ranging from bungalows to barns, houses to hog pens. All sales were cash-and-carry.

The Hopkins home and eight surrounding outbuildings brought in the pitiful sum of $1,001.50, far less than the $20,000 they needed to begin anew. A commissioner review on August 1 re-calibrated the Hopkins property value to $66,000. The public never knew what happened at the end of the Hopkins' petition review. Local newspapers kept quiet about the outcome.

The Hopkins farm destruction began in earnest. "Under the terms of the land sale, everything must be removed from the premises on or before Aug. 26," the News Journal declared. "It was announced, however, that all the buildings on the Hopkins property must be removed by Aug. 12, because the grading is reaching that point." They were the last and most troublesome of the landowners to settle their affairs. Forty-nine properties were already sold, completely free of any lingering liabilities. Yet, despite open ground elsewhere, construction crews seemed eerily poised to target the Hopkins family. Was there a hushed directive to rapidly raze their buildings? The state seemed engaged in a shadowy bid to forestall the looming threat of a court ruling. Authorities raced against time to avoid further complications. Bulldozers completely erased the farm by mid-August, leaving an empty void where life and prosperity had once flourished.

By October, John and Florence Hopkins had found a new home at Kanmichko Farms, near Elkton, Maryland. The harsh experience of being uprooted from their community took a toll. Additionally, the turmoil of starting anew had a lasting impact. Three years later, in April 1944, John fell seriously ill. This was the same month he first learned about the traumatic upheaval destined to dramatically alter his life. Hopkins went to Baltimore to seek treatment at the world-class University of Maryland Hospital. Despite weeks of extended treatment, his condition only slightly improved. John T. Hopkins, the holdout of Hare's Corner, died on May 6, 1944, at the age of 57.

The story of John and Florence Hopkins poignantly underscores the human cost of progress. Their radical displacement epitomizes the sacrifices of emotional, social, and financial upheaval. John lost more than his farm in the clash between national defense and personal property rights. He surrendered his livelihood, community, and the possibility of growing old. The federal government's war-time decision transformed New Castle County. Modernization's steep price left a swath of winners...and losers.

Page 36 Fort Miles

Among the fort's constructions, the standout was Battery 519, a 420-foot underground bunker with 12-inch coastal defense guns, epitomizing the fort's extensive military infrastructure. Nineteen towers, erected along both the Delaware (15 towers) and New Jersey (4 towers) coastlines, were the eyes of Fort Miles. If tower spotters saw an enemy surface ship, they would roughly triangulate ship coor dinates, then call the battery crew. Plot room soldiers calculated trajectory factors like wind speed and Earth's curvature. Large-caliber guns, including 16-inch and 12-inch batteries, stood ready to thwart any naval incursion. Gunners could fire a 1,100-pound shell up to 15 miles.

Germany declared war on the U.S. four days after Japan's surprise Pearl Harbor attack. 1,200 Nazi U-boats under Admiral Karl Doenitz posed an imminent threat to America's East Coast. The limited effectiveness of the period's sonar technology further intensified this danger. The entire Atlantic seaboard was prey to these "undersea boats." Doenitz's fleet targeted Allied shipping lanes and came ominously close to American shores. The armada was a continuing menace. In the war's early days, German subs sank 25 ships. No U-boat was damaged.

Fort Miles, in response, expanded defensive operations to include anti-submarine measures, making thirty-six types of artillery available. Military personnel coordinated their activities along the Atlantic coast with other defense installations. They worked particularly closely with Fort DuPont and New Jersey's Fort Mott, collectively establishing a robust Delaware Bay line of defense. They operated in multiple capacities throughout the war. Fort Miles functioned as a coastal artillery training outpost and acted as an internment camp for prisoners of war, primarily housing German naval personnel. This dual capacity demonstrated the base's adaptability. The Delaware fort never saw direct combat during the war but maintained strategic importance. Functioning as a deterrent to enemy vessels, the installation sought to prevent disruptions to American shipping and block any infiltrations along the Delaware River.

In late March 1945, Admiral Doenitz dispatched six U-boats, leading America to launch 'Operation Teardrop' on April 24. This U.S. Navy mission, involving four aircraft carriers, 112 planes, and 42 destroyer escorts, aimed to locate and neutralize the lurking U-boats. Intelligence rumors of long-range 'rocket bombs' on these German subs — a potential threat to East Coast cities — drove the urgency. Yet, despite the Navy sinking four U-boats and capturing one in April, U-858 managed to elude the dragnet.

The world celebrated VE Day on May 8, 1945, marking the end of the war in Europe. German Lt. Commander Thilo Bode and his U-858 remained at large for another six days. The rogue ship finally emerged off Cape Henlopen, yielding to the Allied forces formally at Fort Miles. The surrender process was multifaceted. The 57-man crew first submitted to the Marines who boarded the vessel. Following American military branch protocol, the German seamen re-enacted the capitulation for Admiral J.P. Norfleet. Finally, the Kriegsmarine personnel were led ashore to Fort Miles, an Army-operated facility. There, the prisoners were surprised to learn that they had to yield yet again. The base did not formally recognize a Naval concession on Army grounds.

A chapter in history closed with less drama than had characterized the conflict's 1941 beginnings. The event marked the first instance of a foreign power surrendering on U.S. soil since the War of 1812. *Battery "E" gunners photo courtesy Fort Miles Museum and Historical Area; Watch Towers photo Big Dog 91/Flickr; Thilo Bode portrait Official Navy Photo/Delaware Public Archives*

Page 37 Dover Army Airbase

Civilian contractors, with oversight and funding from the CAA, broke ground in March 1941 on Dover Airdrome, the newly named municipal airport, which encompassed three hard-surface runways and one hangar. Progress was slow due to limited funding, but everything changed dramatically following the December 7 Pearl Harbor Japanese bombing. The attack thrust the United States into the war. Within ten days, the Department of War had leased Delaware's three incomplete municipal airports for use as coastal patrol bases in the Eastern Defense Command. Construction requirements at the newly renamed Dover Army Airfield strikingly increased as the country went to war. The Army Corps of Engineers took charge of the efforts, working tirelessly day and night to prepare the facility for wartime operations. Despite these efforts to get the base up and running, early occupants faced numerous hardships. Running water and electricity were not available, forcing work crews to eat from mess kits and rely on civilian facilities for bathing. Unusually heavy rains turned the airfield into marshland, hindering progress and further compounding an already difficult situation.

The first military unit arrived at Dover's new airfield on December 20, 1941. The 112th Observation Squadron of the Ohio National Guard, equipped with O-47 aircraft, conducted anti-submarine patrols along the Delaware Coast. Three B-25 bomber squadrons joined the base in 1942, assuming the anti-submarine mission. In 1943 the Army extended the main runway to 7,000 feet. Subsequently, seven P-47 fighter squadrons arrived to train for their eventual participation in the European theater. Dover Army Airfield took on an additional role in 1944. The Air Technical Service Command selected the base to engineer, develop, and conduct classified air-launched rocket tests. Valuable information gathered from these experiments contributed to the effective deployment of air-to-surface rockets in both the European and Pacific combat theaters.

Following World War II's Allied victory, Dover Army Airfield served as a stopover hub for redirecting troops returning from the European theater. However, by 1946, the Army relegated the facility to caretaker status. The future of Dover Army Airfield became uncertain. Over the long haul, temporary mothballing did not prevent the airstrip from evolving and growing. President Harry S. Truman signed the National Security Act of 1947, officially creating The United States Air Force (USAF). The new military establishment took control of the Dover installation from the United States Army Air Forces in 1950. USAF's commanding general, General George Kenney, changed the name to Dover Air Force Base on January 13, 1948. Today, as a vital component of the national defense infrastructure, Dover Air Force Base has grown to become one of the country's largest Air Force commands. *Aerial photo Hagley Museum & Library*

Page 38 Medal of Honor recipient William Lloyd Nelson

Nelson hoped to transfer to the Ordnance Corps and even entertained dreams of attending Officer Candidate School. They never materialized, however. His division, the Ninth, in fall 1942 received orders to ship out to Africa. He actively participated in the "Operation Torch" invasion force landing in North Africa on November 8th. His unit put ashore at Port Lyautey on French Morocco's Atlantic. Engagement southwest of Gibraltar, marked by limited use of heavy mortars, toughened them for the upcoming Tunisian campaign.

The Sixtieth secured the Port Lyautey landing area and then pressed on to Oran. At Station de Sened, they caught an Italian battalion off guard. Nelson, now a sergeant, commanded such an effective mortar barrage, the entire battalion surrendered. Following a winter of additional training, Nelson's regiment achieved top-notch form. President Roosevelt even reviewed them during an appearance in Casablanca. In April 1943, they prepared for a decisive push toward Bizerte. The regiment, stationed in Sedjenane, received their orders on the night of the 22nd to capture the German-held ridge of Djebel Dardyss, a mountain that dominated the local landscape. The Americans felt that to rid the area of the enemy, Djebel Dardyss would have to be taken and fortified. In preparation for the assault, the U.S. Army had been prepositioning troops and equipment, ensuring they were ready to strike when the orders came.

The Sixtieth advanced under cover from their own artillery. The Americans inched their way up the mountain, with the 2nd Battalion leading the way. Thick undergrowth slowed progress. They were only halfway up the slope by nightfall. Nelson knew the next day would be challenging. "If your number's up, you'll get it," he had once told his worried wife, Rebecca, "no matter what you do. If it isn't up, you'll pull through."

Hitler's army, meantime, realized what the Americans had done in gaining a foothold on Djebel Dardyss and regrouped to stop their advance. The Germans began a thunderous counteroffensive as dawn broke, raining down shells on the Allied troops.

Nelson, the observer for his mortar section, led the artillery to an advanced position, while crawling forward to better scout out the enemy below. Once there, the sergeant saw an opportunity: a large concentration of Nazis moving into position. He relayed the firing instructions, then issued the order for rapid fire as soon as the coordinates lined up. "He directed the laying of a concentrated mortar barrage which successfully halted an initial enemy counterattack," according to his Medal of Honor citation.

Even in the face of intense German fire from all sides, Nelson remained at his post, shifting positions to better direct the mortar fire. Then, he was struck by a grenade and lay wounded and numb on the ground. Rather than seek medical treatment, Nelson pressed on. "With his duty clearly completed, Sergeant Nelson crawled to a still more advanced observation post and continued to direct the fire. Dying of hand-grenade wounds and only fifty yards from the enemy, he encouraged his section to continue their fire, and by doing so took a heavy toll on enemy lives," stated his citation.

Nelson's efforts at Djebel Dardyss, along with those of other brave Americans, gave a great tactical advantage to the American forces. Three weeks later, 275,000 German and Italian soldiers surrendered, thus ending Hitler's North African campaign.

William L. Nelson's Medal of Honor commendation saluted his "priceless inspiration to our Armed Forces" and acknowledged that his sacrifices were "in keeping with the highest traditions of the U.S. Army." *Medal of Honor photo public domain, PD-USGOV-Military award; Nelson photo courtesy Delaware Public Archives*

Page 39 Medal of Honor recipient James Connor

The USS *Samuel Chase* landed James Connor and his battle patrol platoon at the water's edge of Cavalaire-sur-Mer. The Army gave the 36-man corps a critical mission: seize the heights held by German forces. "As we started inland from the water . . . I suddenly noticed a wire just above my head," said Staff Sgt. Herman F. Nevers, leader of the first squad. "I looked back and . . . saw . . . a hanging mine explode and tear the platoon leader into small pieces. The force of the explosion blew Sergeant James P. Connor about ten feet and knocked him flat to the ground. Sergeant Connor received a fragmentation wound on the left side of the neck . . . The commanding officer of the battle patrol told him to go back for aid, but Sergeant Connor refused to go."

Connor's quick actions a few miles up the beach saved his squad. In a crucial moment at a small bridge, a German soldier suddenly appeared. Connor swiftly neutralized the threat. Moments later, a severe mortar barrage engulfed the patrol. Urging his men forward, Connor faced a moment of chaos. The group scattered, some merging with another platoon. Regrouping, the platoon advanced once more with Connor leading the way. A German soldier emerged from a foxhole just thirty feet ahead and shot Connor in the leg. As Connor fell, Nevers fired over him, killing the rifleman. Only about twenty battle patrolmen remained after the dust settled.

A sniper shot Sergeant Connor, wounding him in the left shoulder, the bullet penetrating his back. "'For Christ's sake, Connor,' said Nevers, 'stop and get medical attention for yourself!' The sergeant replied, saying, 'No, they can hit me, but they can't stop me. I'll go until I can't go any farther.' Then he said, 'Nevers, get out there on the right flank and get those men rolling! We've got to clean out these snipers before we can advance farther!' Sergeant Connor told the men, 'If there's only one of us left, we've got to get to that point [the objective] and clean it up, so the guys coming in after us can get in safely with no fire on them.'

"He called and told me to give him a hand to help him to his feet so he could go on with the fight," said Nevers. "I helped him up, but he couldn't stand and fell down again. I wanted to give him first aid, but he wouldn't even let me look at the wound, saying there wasn't time. He told me to take the rest of the men, about fifteen now, and to carry on, and that he hoped he would see me sometime. Sergeant Connor told me that even if I had to get down and dig the bastards out with my bare hands to go ahead and dig them out . . ." The group proceeded to execute Connor's instructions, according to Sergeant Edward G. Collins. "Every man saw that Sergeant Connor was entirely exposed to the enemy fire on the beach road and he didn't back down," Collins said. "The mines were thick, but he told them the only way to get through was to run as fast as possible. He told them that by advancing faster than the Germans could figure their fire data, they would run safely under the mortar fire, but if they stood still, they were goners. When we cleared the mortar fire, and ran into machine gun and additional mortar fire, the men wanted to take cover until help could arrive," said Collins. "But Sergeant Connor told them we had to get our objective, even if only one man got there, because other guys wouldn't even be able to land."

The platoon successfully followed Connor's orders and secured the area, eliminating three or four enemy soldiers and capturing around forty more. "But for the outstanding example set by Sergeant Connor in the face of tremendous odds in fire power and men," said 1st Lt. William K. Dieleman, battle patrol commander, "the critically important mission of the whole battle patrol might have been delayed for a considerable time or might even have failed entirely."

Lt. Gen. Alexander M. Patch awarded James Phillip Connor the Congressional Medal of Honor. In May 1945, President Harry Truman honored him at the White House. Connor returned to Wilmington, where officials ceremoniously presented him with the key to the city. The war left an indelible mark, shaping a lifelong dedication to others serving in the military. Connor went on to work at the Veterans Administration for 34 years before passing away in 1994 at 75. He now rests at Delaware Veterans Memorial Cemetery in Bear.

James Connor's acts of courage on the battlefield represent a monumental tribute to his unconquerable spirit. Our recognition of Connor's story also tacitly extends homage to many others like him who never received similar accolades. *James Connor portrait by Frank E. Schoonover, Delware State Museums Collection; Invasion of Southern France photo courtesy National Museum of the U.S. Navy*

Page 40 Lonely Hearts Murders

For those singles seeking love and connection, lonely-hearts clubs emerged as a beacon of hope. These were not "clubs" at all, but rather classified ads, translating the timeless quest for intimacy into newsprint. Would-be suitors sought to match their attributes and aspirations with kindred spirits. The strongest argument against the romanticized view of lonely-hearts clubs came from visceral, real-life stories that revealed humanity's darker side. One such intrigue revolves around Inez Gertrude Brennan of Dover.

The narrative begins with Charles Wende and his wife traveling back from Florida to New Hampshire in April 1949. They decided to drop by Dover and make an impromptu visit to an old friend, Hugo Schulz. He had told them in December 1948 he was planning to relocate there to be with Inez, his new bride.

However, when the Wendes reached the Brennan farm, Inez coldly greeted them, and rudely denied any knowledge of Schulz. The 45-year-old's demeanor changed when the Wendes explained a connection; she curtly admitted that Schulz had "stopped here briefly."

The vague remark raised the Wendes' suspicions, leading them to Dover's State Police, where they shared their concerns about Inez Brennan. Their apprehensions found an unsettling resonance in recent reports from Sheriff Claude Ruff of Bedford County, Virginia. He was investigating the mysterious disappearance of Wade Wooldridge, a 70-year-old carpenter from Virginia with intentions of meeting his mail-order bride, a certain Mrs. Brennan of Dover. The widow lived with her 16-year-old son Robert, a handsome sophomore at Dover High, and Ray, her stocky, curly-haired 23-year-old son. There was a boarder, Dolly T. Dean. An 18-year-old son, George, was stationed in Texas at Lackland Air Force Base.

Dover State Police wasted no time launching an investigation into Inez Brennan and her mysterious mannerisms. On April 14, 1949, investigators searched for buried bodies on the Brennan farm. As Major James Turner turned his spade into the pigpen's dirt, Robert blurted: "There's no sense digging there. The bodies were removed and taken to the city dump!" Major Turner hustled Inez and her two sons off to the State Police barracks. There, Inez and Ray claimed they had nothing to say. However, Robert had a different response. In the dimly lit room, he started spilling the beans.

He said that the previous October 10th, Wooldridge had arrived at the farm. Brother George had just reported for Air Force duty. "Mother said, 'Nobody will miss him if somebody puts something through his head,'" Robert stated. "She said he had a considerable sum of money on him, and we could use that," according to the court record.

Robert went on: "About 4:45 pm on October 10th I decided to get rid of Mr. Wooldridge. So, I took my 12-gauge shotgun to the barn and put it in the loft. Then we all had supper. "After supper Mr. Wooldridge wanted to see the outside buildings. I took him straight to the barn. While he was looking around, I went to the loft. I shot him in the back of the head as he came up. He rolled to the floor." The clan divided Wooldridge's things and buried his body in the pigpen corral, according to the teenager. On December 27th, Robert and his mother went by train to Concord, New Hampshire. Hugo Schulz met them, and they all went to his farm.

After several pleasant days together, Inez asked Schulz for $1,000 to pay a note on her farm, only to be met with refusal. In response, she first attempted to poison his food with five sleeping pills, then 17 the next day; both without effect. The couple went to town on January 8th to get a marriage license. A night or so later, Inez tried slipping Schulz a dose of arsenic. He took ill for five hours, though he recovered again. The plot took a deadly turn three days later in the barn, when Inez handed her son Robert a gun and directed the barrel at Schulz. When Robert lost his nerve, Inez seized the weapon and fired twice. Schulz fell dead. Mother and son wrapped the body in canvas and stuffed it into a 50-gallon oil drum. Inez wrote to Ray to come north, then sold off Schulz's 400 chickens as well as his farm equipment. When Ray arrived, they loaded the drum and furniture onto a truck and drove to Delaware. In March, they buried Schulz in the pigpen corral beside Wooldridge.

Meantime, Brennan's boarder, Dolly Dean, grew suspicious and moved away, fearing for her own life. She had seen too much and was now a target. Police learned that widow Inez had placed many lonely-hearts club ads. Two earlier contacts lost some money but escaped with their lives. Officers arrested Brennan and sons Robert and Ray on suspicion of murder. Delaware police hauled George back from Texas for questioning. Yes, he remembered October 10th. "Mother told me Mr. Wooldridge had been shot," George recalled. "She said I'd have to get up early the next morning to help bury him."

On the Kent County Court of Oyer and Terminer (today the Kent County Court of Common Pleas) witness stand, Robert said his mother decided to sell the Dover farm in a hurry. So, Inez, Robert, and Ray dug up the bodies and cremated them. Later, Robert said he and Ray had left the ashes in cans at the Dover city dump. The Delaware court admitted several bones and two boxes of ash-filled cans retrieved from the landfill into evidence as Wooldridge's earthly remains. The prosecution called on Richard Ayres of Stone Mountain, Virginia, who identified several articles found on the Delaware farm as those of his grandfather, Wooldridge. Dolly Dean testified she heard a shot, and that Robert told her, "I shot the old man." Dean said Wooldridge did not die immediately and screamed. "We can't have him hollering like that," she heard Inez say. Robert took the gun from the kitchen. Dean remembered another shot. "I finished off the old man. I shot off half his face," Robert told her.

The court entered Robert's confession into evidence despite the defense objection. Inez took the stand and denied telling Robert to kill Wooldridge. Robert gave a new testimony. He claimed that Wooldridge was "getting fresh" with Dolly. When he told the man to leave, he now claimed, Wooldridge pulled a knife on him. Kent County Court charged Robert with murder and named his mother as an accomplice. The court named George and Ray accessories to the crime. Though the jurors found Robert and his mother guilty, they asked mercy for him. The judge sentenced both to life, since Delaware law precluded giving an accomplice a more severe term than the perpetrator. The court sentenced Ray to two years and George to one, following their guilty pleas as accessories. As to Hugo Shulz's murder, Inez and Robert were indicted by New Hampshire's Merrimack County Superior Court.

Their trial began on September 12, 1949, but it soon reached a dead end. Two months later, the local *Concord Monitor* reported, "New Hampshire will have to wait at least 15 years before it can try Mrs. Inez Brennan." The report further stated, "She cannot apply for a commutation of her [Delaware] sentence until she has served 15 years." Brennan did complete that portion of her punishment. After that, she was obligated to report for parole for the rest of her life. However, in 1976, she was released from this requirement. Brennan was never brought to a second New Hampshire trial. Inez Gertrude Brennan died age 80, a free woman, in 1984.

This chilling episode is a stark reminder of the perils that sometimes lurk behind the promises of connection. While the human heart may yearn for companionship, the seat of desire also harbors the capacity for unspeakable cruelty.

Page 41 Nylon in Seaford

Carothers and his dedicated team discovered nylon in 1935 after years of relentless polymerization inquiry. While this breakthrough signified a remarkable achievement, the troubled chemist's private battles overshadowed his success. The contrast between personal despair and the triumphant reception of nylon painted a heartrending picture when Wallace Carothers committed suicide in April 1937.

The fiber itself debuted at the 1939 New York World's Fair, setting the stage for widespread adoption. Eager to capitalize on this innovation, DuPont embarked on a meticulous site-selection process for a new production facility. The company evaluated 14 potential locations before deciding. Key factors in the process included water supply, available workforce, and transportation infrastructure. The company opted for a 609-acre site along Seaford's Nanticoke River for their plant. Carothers' brainchild dramatically reshaped Seaford when DuPont came to town.

The selection ignited spontaneous celebrations: fireworks lit the sky, marching bands from Seaford and three nearby towns filled the air with music, and grown men wept openly on the streets at the prospect of much-needed employment. "Seaford is a 'Cinderella Town'!" enthused one Philadelphia radio commentator.

Construction on the plant commenced in March 1939 and was completed within 14 months. December arrived with approximately 850 workers joining the operation. Some even hailed from distant Maryland towns such as Pocomoke City and Cambridge. Together, they spun the world's first nylon yarn.

The new synthetic polymer initially appeared in toothbrush bristles before becoming a more affordable alternative to silk in bridal veils. On May 15, 1940, the day nylon stockings debuted in the US, consumers bought 800,000 pairs. DuPont's "miracle fiber" quickly adorned millions of American women's legs. The Seaford plant operated ceaselessly during the inaugural year, churning out enough fiber for an impressive 64 million pairs of nylon stockings by year's end. DuPont recognized the need for worker housing and subsequently purchased 153 acres in Seaford to build homes for an expanding workforce.

Nylon's utility transcended hosiery. The company took advantage of the polymer's versatility, using the fabric in parachutes, seatbelts, uniforms, food wrappings, life rafts, and tents. The material's rigid form came to be used in guitar strings and even gun barrels. "Artificial silk" found crucial new applications in World War II. With war's onset, the Seaford plant transitioned towards supporting the military. After the attack on Pearl Harbor, the U.S. government allocated all nylon production for critical wartime supplies—ranging from parachutes to airplane tire cord. Allied troops relied heavily on nylon, creating such a demand that American authorities banned use for stockings until peacetime.

The war effort drove DuPont plants in Seaford and Martinsville, Virginia, to manufacture approximately 80 million pounds of nylon yarn and "flakes." Skilled women kept positions fully staffed while men were at the front lines. Demand exceeded supply when nylon stockings reappeared after the war. This disparity led to "nylon riots." Eager customers overwhelmed stores, vividly demonstrating nylon's impact on everyday life. In one infamous incident, 40,000 Pittsburgh women queued up for just 13,000 pairs.

Within decades, Seaford firmly established a reputation as the "Nylon Capital of the World." By 1969, the plant employed 3,400 workers. DuPont's nylon production reigned as the company's most lucrative endeavor for over half a century. However, boom towns exhibit a fleeting character. Even robust industries can wane, leading to shifts in economic fortunes. DuPont eventually sold the Seaford plant in 2004, moving production to locales with cheaper labor.

"DuPont supported a lot of ancillary businesses, from machine shops to cleaning services," noted State Representative Danny Short in 2015. "It was a hub of employment that provided us with everything, including one of the best school districts in the state."

Nylon's dramatic effect on Seaford illuminates the positive intersection of material science innovation with economic opportunity. Originating from the ingenuity of a lone chemist, nylon's technological breakthrough caught the attention of a visionary corporation and fueled immediate success. Such combined efforts both revolutionized the economy and fundamentally changed the fabric of everyday life.
Two interior photos of Seaford Plant courtesy Delaware Public Archives; External plant photo courtesy Hagley Museum and Library

Page 42 Pauline Young Library

Mary, the mother, and Alice, the aunt, actively participated as members of the National Association for the Advancement of Colored People (NAACP). Their example prompted Pauline to join the organization at the early age of twelve.

The segregated University of Delaware blocked Pauline's attendance, but she refused to be denied further schooling. Instead, she took the train to Philadelphia, where she studied at the University of Pennsylvania. In 1921, Penn granted her a Bachelor of Arts in Education. Post-graduation, Pauline bounced around for half a decade in several places. She taught history at Virginia's Huntington High School in Newport News and worked as a member of the press staff for Alabama's Tuskegee Institute.

Circling back to Wilmington, the hometown girl took a position as an instructor of history and Latin at her high school alma mater. Howard High later gave Pauline charge of a small library that a board of education member, Dr. Henry Clay Stevenson, had donated from his own collection. Colleagues recognized her talent in managing the catalog and urged Pauline to further pursue library science. She earned a master's degree from Columbia University in 1935, a credential that paved the way for future eminence.

Pauline converted the Howard High School library into a hub that transcended community expectations. The facility offered reading programs, neighborhood discussions, and educational outreach under her resourceful stewardship. These events offered Wilmington's Black community an unprecedented platform. Her library played a vital role for a marginalized population, fostering intellectual growth and civic engagement. Pauline brought notable African American speakers and artists to the library. This dedicated educator continued to teach history and social studies. These subjects gave her a springboard from which to imbue the next generation with a sense of historical context and social justice.

Pauline contributed to Henry Clay Reed's three-volume "Delaware: A History of the First State" (1947), with a piece entitled "The Negro in Delaware: Past and Present" in response to the need for more histories about African Americans. This work became one of the first comprehensive written accounts of Black contributions to Delaware history.

A tireless advocate for civil rights and social justice, Pauline played a prominent role in several organizations, including the League of Women Voters and the American Federation of Teachers. She once chaired the NAACP's state education committee, where she actively championed integration. This educator/advocate's expertise in both realms made her a key figure in the movement to desegregate Delaware schools. "Democracy is a living thing, kept alive only by its exercise and the eternal vigilance of all its constituents," thundered a

1953 Letter to the Editor of the *News Journal*. This expression of her passion echoed the growing national sentiment and contributed to the momentum leading to the landmark 1954 *Brown v. Board of Education* case.

Pauline continued her advocacy work after retiring from Howard High School in 1961. Her commitment to education and civil rights took her to Jamaica with the Peace Corps from 1962-1964. There she trained librarians and cataloged books. Numerous awards recognized both lifelong and extensive dedication, including her 1983 induction into the Delaware Women's Hall of Fame. "I stay mad," she told the *News Journal* shortly before her death. "And I'm damn mad at any injustice." Pauline A. Young died in 1991, but the historian's gift — the power of education, community engagement, and principled activism — endures.

Page 43 Polio Epidemic

Poliomyelitis ("polio" for short) posed a daunting challenge to mankind for thousands of years. The American medical community started earnestly combating this terrible scourge early in the twentieth century. Austrian Karl Landsteiner and Erwin Popper confirmed a virus as polio's cause in 1908, thereby providing a cornerstone for vaccine development.

Delaware began requiring doctors in 1915 to report polio occurrences to the Bureau of Vital Statistics. Furthermore, incorporated town health boards decreed, for the duration of the illness, polio-infected households display a red quarantine sign on the front door. The summer of 1916 saw major outbreaks of "infantile paralysis," as the disease was then called, erupt in nearby New York and New Jersey. Delaware, in response, implemented stringent measures. Children under 16 from these states were barred as a quarantine strategy. This new, menacing outbreak surged nationwide.

The iron lung's invention in 1928 gave fresh hope to victims and their families. This mechanical respirator supported breathing when patients lost control of their muscles. However, the device also exacted a considerable toll on users. For instance, in 1936, a Middletown teenage boy afflicted with respiratory failure spent five continuous weeks clamped into an Emerson Respirator. Even so, he had to return for multiple sessions over the following weeks, despite his original extended stay.

Wilmington suffered a polio outbreak in 1944, followed by another particularly harsh one a few years later. In mid-August of 1947, the city closed all city pools as the body count rose to 37. Within days the *Morning News* reported 93 affected people. Schools near Wilmington delayed their openings by several weeks. A team of epidemiologists descended on the city in September to scrutinize the epidemic. They were part of a study by the National Foundation for Infantile Paralysis.

"In Wilmington," reported the *Morning News*, "many cases occurred where there was open sewage. Children were said to have gone swimming in polluted water. Samples ... are being studied," continued the newspaper. "DDT was sprayed in part of the city to kill possible insect carriers." Wilmington General Hospital's Doris Memorial Unit counted 122 cases before the 1947 outbreak subsided.

Columnist Bill Frank reflected, in the summer of 1949, on his city's fearful upheaval. He debunked the misconception that polio was often found in open sewer areas and emphasized that the disease remained a mystery. Parents were scared when told their child had polio. Modern-day science eased the blow. Youngsters still had a good chance of resuming normal activities. Frank pointed out at least 75% of polio cases resulted in full or near-full recovery, which provided some comfort to anxious mothers and fathers. He acknowledged that while the fight against polio continued, the community's mindset had drastically changed: "They are not as frightened as they were two years ago and are more calm than the previous year." Bill Frank ended his column on a hopeful note, stating, "Swimming pools were kept open this summer. Polio patient ambulances were used for other contagious cases. Victims are being admitted to general hospitals and not all necessarily to a contagious building. The fight against polio continues in the laboratories and research centers, but here at home, at least in Wilmington, we've just about won the fight against the fear of polio."

Wilmington, as well as other parts of Delaware and the rest of the world, would have to wait six more years for medical victory. Finally, Dr. Jonas Salk provided a godsend, developing the first successful polio vaccine at the University of Pittsburgh. Waves of relief flooded through every household. This revolutionary medical breakthrough became known as the inactivated polio vaccine (IPV) or simply the Salk Vaccine. The iron lung could finally, and forever, be retired. *Polio molecular model: Science Photo Library; overview of polio ward courtesy Science History Images/Alamy Stock Photo*

Page 44 Delaware Memorial Bridge

Frank V. du Pont served as the State Highway Commission chairman from 1922 to 1949. Coleman du Pont's son (a luminary in highway construction,) inherited his father's foresight. Frank envisioned the groundbreaking overpass as more than a physical conduit. Instead, he saw the project as a catalyst for long-range economic development, a means for shaping the region's destiny.

A unified Delaware General Assembly gave the nod to the undertaking in May 1945, as did the New Jersey Highway Department. Congress signed off on July 13, 1946, and detailed planning for the building of the dual span promptly began. The new crossing would honor both Delaware and New Jersey World War II heroes. Designers developed blueprints for the massive foundation piers, ensuring the utmost safety at reasonable cost. The State Highway Department issued $25 million worth of underwriting bonds. They later repaid private investors via toll revenues.

Eugene Reybold, Bridge Division engineer, led seafloor tests to ensure the foundation's strength and stability. "Improved sampling devices and methods were employed, many for the first time," reported Reybold. Findings showed absence of bedrock at a 400-foot depth. Therefore, the State Highway Commission announced that the bridge had to be constructed using the "float-in method." This technique works well in deep water or unstable soil conditions where traditional approaches are not feasible. Engineers had built the renowned San Francisco-Oakland Bay Bridge (1936) in the same way.

Meanwhile, acquiring land for the bridge's approach involved lengthy landowner negotiations. The Laws of Delaware 1935 established Highway Department rules. Subsequent 1943 legislation permitted land acquisition through condemnation when negotiations failed. However, the pushback from local citizens, alarmed by the specter of a government-enforced land grab, led to Delaware's 1945 "bridge crossing act" amendment, which sought to safeguard their properties against the overreach of eminent domain. This included a citizen's right to seek damages before an appropriate commission. Prominent owners along the bridge path made outright seizure politically and socially unpalatable. The Highway Department, keen on maintaining a favorable image among the public, actively sought a collaborative approach. This strategy both preserved positive perceptions and fostered mutual respect.

Pittsburgh's Dravo Corporation submitted the lowest bid when the state solicited proposals in December 1947 for two tower-supporting piers plus two bridge anchorages. Their estimate surpassed the State Highway Department's cost projections, raising financial viability concerns. Delaware's treasury explored financing in February 1948 via an insurance company consortium. However, these bond underwriters preferred to invest their funds in housing projects.

Merritt, Chapman & Scott, Inc. bid to construct tower piers and anchorage foundations, contingent on the state selling 75% of a proposed bond subscription by July 23. Delaware successfully met the deadline, ensuring the project's financial viability. With this hurdle cleared, construction in 1949 progressed smoothly. The two main anchorages were successfully cast, and the erection of piers atop them proceeded on schedule. Pittsburgh's American Bridge Company, awarded the steelwork contract, promptly produced 8,000 tons of steel.

By August 10, 1950, the project achieved a milestone as workers spun the first of two 218-wire-strand suspension cables, each of which would span the crossing and connect to the tops of the towers at either end. That assembly took two months, with operations running round-the-clock, except on high wind days. Work proceeded swiftly despite slight setbacks in 1951 due to icy winter conditions. The steel framework anchoring the roadway was in place by March. Vertical suspenders (hangers) connected to the two main cables stabilized the deck. Electricians fitted the bridge by May with lighting and toll systems.

Officials prepared for the Delaware Memorial Bridge's grand inauguration by mid-summer. The new structure was the sixth-longest main suspension span in the world. The dedication ceremony attracted widespread attention, taking place on August 16, 1951. Attendees included Governor Alfred Driscoll of New Jersey and the Governor of Delaware, Elbert N. Carvel. They, and other prominent figures, hailed the bridge as a national symbol of progress and engineering prowess. J. Gordon Smith, chairman of the Delaware State Highway Department, cut the ribbon, and traffic began to flow.

The bridge, costing $43,900,000, stretched a mile across the water from Pigeon Point, Delaware near Wilmington to Deep Water Point near Pennsville, New Jersey. The robust design featured an 86-foot-wide deck encompassing four traffic lanes, two shoulders, and adjacent sidewalks. The thoroughfare is the regional nexus for long-distance travelers driving the Washington—Boston corridor. On November 15, 1951, workers completed the 120-mile-long New Jersey Turnpike, which coupled to the Delaware Memorial Bridge's eastern terminus. The western end links to Route 95, serving Baltimore and points south.

Delaware's largest elevated causeway epitomizes the vision, ambition, and tenacity of many imaginative creators. This monumental achievement successfully harnessed the vast watery expanse between the two shores of Delaware Bay. The elevated pathway holds the distinguished rank of being among the most heavily traveled of American suspension bridges. This grand east-west connector marks a defining moment in the region's transportation history. *Photo of workers on girders: Peter Stackpole/Life Pictures; Bridge aerial: Delaware Public Archives/State Highway Department Photograph Collection; Governor on speaking podium: Delaware Public Archives*

Page 45 University of DE Desegregated

The NAACP in the 1930s started to expose serious deficiencies in Black Delaware schools. This effort overlapped with the Great Migration (1916-1970). During that half-century, approximately six million fled the Jim Crow South. Such a mass movement resulted in an unprecedented concentration in northern cities like Wilmington.

Serious legal challenges to *Plessy* met with only modest successes throughout the 1940s. The year 1950 finally witnessed three landmark victories spearheaded by the NAACP's Legal Defense and Education Fund (LDEF). The LDEF actively searched for potential cases to challenge *Plessy*, focusing on southern and border states with explicit segregation mandates. This approach led directly to the NAACP launching the breakthrough 1950 case of *Parker v. the University of Delaware*.

Ten African American students, denied admission on racial grounds, sought legal recourse under the auspices of famed attorney Louis Redding in Delaware's Chancery Court. Although the court is primarily recognized for expertise in corporate law, the body also holds jurisdiction over many civil rights litigations.

Redding, the first Black person admitted to the state bar, in 1932, argued the case before Vice Chancellor Collins Seitz. The NAACP aimed to leverage Seitz's beliefs. The judge was known for his impartiality on racial matters. Wilmington's Junior Chamber of Commerce honored him with the 1949 Young Man of the Year award. In accepting the accolade, he stepped forward "as the representative of those many people who are striving in innumerable ways to make the 'brotherhood of man' more nearly a reality."

"While I appreciate that, in part, the award is in recognition of my activities in the legal field, nevertheless, I like to think I was chosen in recognition of my efforts in helping to promote the cause of racial and religious tolerance in our community." He concluded by emphasizing the importance to him of such work. "It is my firm conviction that, as a long-range proposition, the preservation of our democracy is dependent upon the substantial realization of this ideal."

Redding joined forces with LDEF lawyer Jack Greenberg for this crucial battle. The collaboration, given their methodical approach and shared dedication to justice, underpinned a strong professional respect between them. *Parker v. University of Delaware* highlighted educational disparities between Delaware State College and the University of Delaware. Louis Redding focused on systemic discrimination that went far beyond college admission, particularly Delaware State's underfunding and lack of national accreditation. He handled the legwork and screened local witnesses. Meanwhile, Greenberg focused on coordinating the Parker strategy with LDEF.

The lawyers did meticulous legal research and preparation prior to standing before Vice Chancellor Seitz. The judge rigorously examined the "separate but equal" doctrine. His ruling stated Delaware's educational facilities were indeed separate, but they were not equal.

In a groundbreaking decision, the court ordered the University of Delaware to desegregate. The university grudgingly complied, making it one of the first American colleges to undertake this monumental step. Jack Greenberg observed, "Although Louis had to campaign to persuade qualified Black applicants to enter the university to capitalize on his victory, the case did have an impact in Delaware." This action foreshadowed the 1954 *Brown v. Board of Education* decision. (Oliver Brown had originally filed a 1951 class-action suit against the Board of Education of Topeka, Kansas.)

In Delaware, the NAACP pursued two more landmark cases: *Bulah v. Gebhart* and *Belton v. Gebhart*. Sarah Bulah first took her own legal action. Then, a group of parents, led by Ethel Belton, filed a separate case. Both sought to name the State Board of Education as the principal defendant. However, when suing a Delaware state entity, the plaintiff must serve a summons directly on the agency's principal officer, in these instances Francis B. Gebhart.

Both cases centered on parents advocating for their Black children's attendance at all-white neighborhood schools in Claymont and Hockessin. Louis Redding teamed up once more with Jack Greenberg. Again, they ended up in Delaware's Court of Chancery. Vice Chancellor Seitz this time stated that although he could not overturn segregation, he could determine, as he had in the Parker case, that the conditions were not "separate but equal."

He noted that band-aid fixes could not prevent the ongoing harm to the children. Judge Seitz pointed out that the evidence showed state-imposed segregation made education for Black students in Delaware "substantially inferior." He stressed that learning conditions paled in comparison to those available to white students who were "otherwise similarly situated."

Consequently, Seitz ordered the admission of the Black students to the named white schools. Delaware Attorney General Albert W. James, on behalf of Gebhart, appealed the decision to the State Supreme Court and lost.

Judge Seitz's decision was a victory for the plaintiffs, yet limited in scope, not applying statewide, nor delivering a sweeping blow to Delaware segregation. Undeterred, the Gebhart defendants escalated their fight to the U.S. Supreme Court. The Belton and Bulah lawsuits would join four other state level NAACP cases, resulting in the 1954 watershed *Brown v. Board of Education* ruling.

The Delaware cases represented major strides. Even so, continuing inequalities trace directly to the misguided *Plessy v. Ferguson* doctrine. The uphill struggles faced by Black students demonstrate eradicating systemic discrimination demands sustained efforts, both legal and societal. *Photo of Collins Seitz courtesy of the Seitz Family; Photo of Louis Redding courtesy First State Blog-Delaware.gov*

Page 46 Amish, Mennonites & Dunkards

The late arrival of the Amish could be attributed to a range of factors. Economic conditions, such as land availability and pricing, play a determining role in community relocation decisions. Furthermore, existing social and religious networks elsewhere could have kept the Amish in areas where they had already established communities. Factors like religious freedom and community tolerance are important for minority religious groups when considering where to establish new settlements.

J.K. Miller, one of Kent County's first Amish settlers, wrote to *The Budget*, the national Amish newsletter, of his new home in Delaware: "It is beautiful level country, no stones, land easily cultivated. Fine farms can be had for $30 an acre." Wrote another: "We would like to see more of our people here. We think this is good country."

The Amish began settling in Kent County. Their enduring tradition of using one-horse buggies stood as a vivid symbol of their commitment to a simpler, more focused way of life. The Amish community decided against car ownership for a multitude of reasons. Cars offered individuals the ability to travel, thus distancing them from their homes. Moreover, the ease of getting about exposed young people to urban environments often linked to vice. These collective issues were perceived to pose a threat to community cohesion. Buggies, by contrast, symbolize a deep-rooted commitment to humility and simplicity.

Amish children, even into the late 1990s, learned the same basic subjects as their parents and grandparents in the one-room schoolhouse—often from the same textbooks. This stands in stark contrast to neighboring state schools, which rush to keep students on the cutting edge with updated curricula. "It is this kind of leveling in the Amish experience that sustains the culture," noted Conrad L. Kanagy, an associate sociology professor at Elizabethtown College, 20 miles from Lancaster, Pennsylvania.

Critics argue the Amish deprive their children of higher education and modern technology. They believe Amish youths cannot make informed choices without exposure to the outside world. The Amish response is that their children are free to leave the community to explore what the world has to offer—after eighth grade and before their adult baptism. The baptism, usually between 18 and 21, is when they make a lifetime commitment to the "ordnung," the passed down rules of the Amish.

The Amish divide themselves into Church Amish and House Amish groups. The former, sometimes called "New Order" Amish, worship in church buildings, and some subgroups permit electricity in their homes as well as gasoline-powered tractors. Amish customs regarding beards also vary—some Church Amish men trim their beards while more traditional House Amish do not. Overall, Church Amish tend to follow slightly more relaxed customs compared to the stricter "Old Order" or House Amish.

You can tell House Amish property, meantime, by the bright paint on the farmstead buildings. Their taste in color, inherently brilliant, is applied to dress styles as well. House Amish convene for worship in a community member's home. The gathering follows a rotation, allowing each household to host worship about once a year. The service lasts from approximately 8 am until noon, incorporating both sermons and prayers. The lessons are Bible recapitulations. The host treats all to a magnificent feast after the service concludes.

The community's wedding practices add another layer to these deeply rooted customs. Courtship and marriage involve a distinct set of rituals. A young man, after deciding to propose, first informs the church deacon of his intentions. The deacon then discusses the matter with the young lady's father. If both parties agree, a wedding ceremony takes place, typically Tuesday, Wednesday, or Thursday. Those days of the week are relatively open for various tasks, allowing weddings to fit more easily into the farming routine. This schedule is particularly convenient in late fall and early spring, before the onset of intensive outdoor work.

The work crew needs a full day to prepare and clean. Weddings are not celebrated on Mondays and Saturdays, as it is considered sacrilegious to have to work or clean on Sundays. Friday is pie-day, the day to bake for the upcoming Sunday and following week. Neighbors gather for an extravagant celebration lasting from morning until the next day, featuring an array of foods from roast geese to shoo-fly pies to heaps of mashed potatoes. The beverages include wine specially made by the bride's father from dandelions or berries and stored from the time of her birth.

While Amish wedding rituals involve elaborate preparations and a focus on community involvement, they are but one reflection of the diverse traditions among Anabaptist groups in Delaware. This diversity is further exemplified by the Dunkards, another faction whose own customs and settlement history contribute to the rich tapestry of the region's cultural heritage.

Around 1904, the Dunkards settled east of Greenwood in Oakley and Owens Station. Farming is their occupation, and like the Amish they have bolstered the area's agricultural yield. They emphasize fiscal responsibility and innovative farming. The Dunkards resemble the Amish as they exit their worship, the women wearing black bonnets and carrying their Bibles—then they step into automobiles.

Mennonites have also carved out their niche among the other two Delaware Anabaptist sects, bringing with them a unique approach to life. The Mennonite origin in the state dates to the mid-17th century, long before the Amish or Dunkards set foot in Kent County. They tried in 1662 to colonize a 25-member community around Lewes called Plockhoy, under Dutch protection. Power struggles between the Dutch and the British over area sovereignty doomed the little settlement. Survivors fled to Germantown in Philadelphia.

In 1913-1914, Valentine Bender and William Tressler, brothers-in-law and Mennonites from Garrett County, Maryland, moved to the Dunkard community in Owen Station and Oakley. They started organizing Sunday meetings in farmhouses. Eventually, they established their own churches and schools in Greenwood and Cannon.

The three Anabaptist communities differ widely in their policies on excommunication and shunning of former members. Specifically, by 1930, the Amish instituted strict social ostracism of excommunicated individuals, meant to isolate them from the community. The Men nonites, however, maintained a narrower, church-focused excommunication that only impacted spiritual standing and not broader social interaction. The Dunkard community has traditionally emphasized reconciliation and restoration over punitive measures.

The Anabaptists are but a few of the many pillars of Delaware's religious and cultural landscape. Striving to harmonize tradition with the demands of modern life, they offer valuable insights into the balancing act between past and present. *Photo: Steven Oney/Flickr*

Page 47 First Television Station

The investment gave Delaware audiences access to Philadelphia area professional sports news and commentary. WDEL became this affiliate during the Golden Age of Radio, carrying NBC dramas, comedies, sports, news, game shows, soap operas, and big bands.

WDEL built on the company's radio success and launched a TV station in 1949. This leveraged their connection with NBC Radio, paving the way for WDEL-TV to promptly become an NBC-TV network associate. The new division also carried programming from the Du-Mont Television Network.

Delaware's first television station flickered to life from Wilmington's Talleyville neighborhood. WDEL-TV broadcasters sent their first signal on June 30, 1949. A world of variety, reach, and visual content opened, and audiences could now watch live NBC programming.

WDEL-TV faced technical issues operating on only 1,000 watts. Viewers outside Wilmington struggled with fluctuating reception due to strong interfering signals from WJZ-TV in New York and WMAL-TV in Washington, D.C.

Early adopters in Wilmington regularly grappled with viewing issues such as a picture without sound, or vice versa. The period's clumsy, user-unfriendly television sets often required the services of "set technicians." They, much like the era's doctors, made house calls.

WDEL-TV broadcast a test pattern every afternoon from 2 to 3 p.m. to mitigate these hardships. This allowed viewers to "tune their sets," thus increasing the possibility of a better reception for the evening's shows. From early on, the station's lineup mirrored today's familiar TV formats and schedules. Popular NBC productions such as *Howdy Doody, Hopalong Cassidy*, and the *Olsen & Johnson* comedy show topped the programming slate.

WDEL launched an FM station in 1950—93.7 WDEL-FM—which simulcast the AM station's programming. Radio tastes gradually changed, and WDEL transitioned to a full-service format featuring news, sports, and middle-of-the-road popular music. To enable stronger signal transmission, WDEL-TV upgraded their FCC license in 1951 from the lower frequency channel 7 to the higher wattage channel 12. In 1954, WDEL-TV noticed the dynamic radio personality Joe Pyne, who captivated WILM viewers with his sharp wit and provocative style, and subsequently poached him from the local competing studio. Today, Pyne is known as the first "talk radio" star.

WDEL-TV's new platform elevated the station's profile among viewers and brought the channel an unprecedented level of attention. Paul F. Harron (owner of Philadelphia's WIBG) purchased the TV outlet from Steinman for a reported $3.7 million in March 1955. Harron renamed the station after himself with the call letters WPFH. Joe Pyne, meantime, left in 1956 to explore opportunities in Los Angeles, where he continued to establish industry fame.

Back in New York, NBC dropped Channel 12's affiliation and WPFH had to run as an independent station. A year later, in March 1957, Harron sold Channel 12 to Storer Broadcasting for $5.6 million and threw in WIBG to sweeten the deal. When Storer bought WPFH, they changed the name to WVUE-TV.

Pyne returned in early 1958 to host late-night talk, boosting the station's ratings thirtyfold. The Joe Pyne Show solidified WVUE's reputation in the television landscape. Despite the ratings boost from Pyne's show, WVUE faced financial difficulties. In August, Storer Broadcasting acquired a Milwaukee affiliate, thereby exceeding the FCC's ownership limit for a single company. This necessitated the sale or shutdown of WVUE to comply with the FCC's seven-station limit. With no buyers forthcoming, Storer Broadcasting ceased WVUE's operations on September 13, 1958, and relinquished the license to the FCC on December 18th of the same year.

WVUE-TV, launched as WDEL on June 30, 1949, chalked up over nine years of broadcasting before closing the doors. This period underscored a legacy of perseverance and innovation. The modest station, beginning with just 1,000 watts and a dedicated team, reshaped Delaware's broadcast experience, one home at a time. *Motorola ad photo, television program ads: public domain; Howdy Doody puppet photo: National Museum of American History*

Page 48 Mancus Club

In 1948, Mary Ann Wright teamed up with fellow community member, Agnes Perrone, a polio survivor, and four additional founders. Together, they spearheaded the creation of what would later evolve into the Mancus Foundation. Members focused on reshaping support and meeting the social, recreational, and transportation needs for marginalized citizens.

The team aimed to foster community advocacy "to help the handicapped help themselves." A few months after the group's founding, their compassion resonated with other Wilmington residents, drawing in 25 philanthropic associate members. This enlargement emphasized the growing recognition and support the club received from the wider community. Base membership, meanwhile, grew to 35 people, encompassing a range of disabilities including those with visual issues.

Wright established a series of weekly radio programs in June 1949. Her broadcasts shared the club's objectives and activities with a much wider audience. On her program, Wright shed light on a troubling school-related challenge: the substantial burden of $100 per week in transportation costs for Wilmington's impaired students.

To address this, she proposed that the Mancus Club could provide affordable, specially equipped busing for those children. Wright, a member of the Women's Insurance Club of Delaware, leveraged her connections there. This network responded with a generous donation, underwriting the busing program by the end of 1949. "Your child's future depends upon the efforts you make in demanding his rights for education," Wright declared, "which no one can doubt is and always will be of the greatest importance to the disabled."

Nor did Wright shy away from voicing her support for statutory change. She focused club attention in early 1951 on House Bill No. 67. The proposed legislation aimed to build better educational facilities for students in need. "The members of the club are shining examples of what disabled persons can do if given the opportunity," she said once the bill had passed.

The Mancus Club, striving to balance serious endeavors with leisure, prioritized hosting an annual Christmas party/variety show. These festivities attracted public figures including Mayor James F. Hearn and Superintendent of Public Safety, A. J. Kavanaugh.

The club's growth accelerated after the founders appointed a board of directors and officers, steering the organization towards more ambitious goals. The board envisioned building a Wilmington clubhouse for physically challenged persons—a place where the community's potential could be publicly exhibited. They started hosting benefit revues by May 1951, directing all proceeds towards this goal-oriented project. Their building fund reached $2,500 by October. The club promptly announced a drive to collect an additional $5,000. The 1952 fundraising target dramatically expanded to $25,000.

Wright brought the goal to life by creating 50 oversized piggy banks for January distribution to local civic clubs. These organizations embraced the concept, with many members creatively decorating the piggy banks using paint, ribbons, and bows.

During the first count of coins from 36 returned piggy banks, every coin was counted correctly by the club's blind members! Entrusting the least likely candidates epitomized the club's core principle. Onlookers saw their success was absolute.

Public figure endorsements, like NBC's songstress Kate Smith, and generous donations from a wide swath of Wilmington organizations began to bolster funds. The club's fundraising crescendoed with Mancus Club Week, an event capped by a star-studded show.

They reached the goal after twelve years of tireless fundraising, organizing countless variety shows and ceaseless public campaigns. By 1964, the organization had incorporated into the Mancus Foundation, signaling the club was committed to formal governance and management. The new foundation purchased a vacant Wilmington recreation center at Danby and Jessup Streets for $80,000.

The building needed extensive renovations. "We're holding an open house instead of having a show this year," Wright triumphantly told the public. "The friends who have patronized our shows over the years can come see what they've contributed."

The Mancus Foundation had blossomed since the early days of convening in Wright's living room. The Delaware Women's Hall of Fame honored Mary Ann Wright's lifelong advocacy by inducting her as an inaugural member in 1981.

The enduring impact of the Mancus Foundation lies in a continuing statewide commitment to enhancing the lives of disabled individuals. This diverse organization achieves professionalism by fostering the independence of those with special needs, making sure they have ongoing community involvement. *photos of Mary Ann Wright and Agnes Perrone courtesy Mancus Foundation, Inc.*

Page 49 Union Strikes

Meanwhile, Don A. Loftus, a Miami-based developer, was consumed by a golden dream: the creation of Delaware's first modern shopping mall. He broke ground on the $20 million project in February 1951. The Merchandise Mart at Edge Moor started to take shape with sprawling foundations giving rise to gleaming steel girders.

Yet, a foreboding challenge emerged. Tensions brewed within the construction crews. Storms of labor unrest loomed. However, Loftus remained undaunted. His determination to persist was unshakable, impervious to any obstacle or opposition.

John Turulski, business agent of Wilmington's plumber's union, got wind of the unrest. Hardheaded Loftus stoked the 42-year-old plumber's appetite. Turulski had been at the helm of two successful, albeit smaller, union organizing drives. This new situation was a tempting and potentially career-changing moment.

Orchestrating a professional picket line at Merchandise Mart would rally the workers, but John had bigger fish to fry. He was hungry to be in the media spotlight shining on such a high-profile construction site.

Turulski set up picket lines in October 1951 at the construction site's west wing. He targeted general contractor Frederick & Jones. He unequivocally demanded full union representation for fellow workers. Though the firm employed some union labor via subcontractors, Turulski told the news, "Our objective is to keep picketing until Frederick & Jones hire a completely unionized crew."

A former president of the Building Trades Council (BTC) union, Turulski understood the power of unity. He galvanized BTC support. Plumbers, bricklayers, and iron workers were among those answering Turulski's call. United, they voiced their objections to salary conditions. "Bricklayers can't lay brick unless the ironwork is up," he stated. His admonitions reminded everyone of the intricate web that bound their trades together.

For his part, Loftus, chairman of the Wilmington Merchandise Mart Corporation, pointed out that the dispute was between the contractors and the council. He told newspapers he was keeping "hands off."

Picket lines disrupted operations. Frederick & Jones bowed to union demands. Then Turulski shifted to the Petrillo Brothers, sole dissenting sub-contractor. Union workers balked at handling "non-union concrete" and pushed for the cement manufacturer's support. "The council is seeking a meeting with Petrillo," the organizer said. He was quick to add, "The picketing will continue." Petrillo's cement mixers kept crossing the line. Many Wilmington area construction sites, watching Turulski's strike, dropped Petrillo and switched to other suppliers.

Despite the concrete maker's unwavering Merchandise Mart deliveries, Turulski's protesters persisted with their demonstrations. This relentless effort led to a stalemate by October's end.

November saw a temporary resolution of the Building Trades Council—Petrillo Brothers standoff, effectively ending work stoppage. Their mutual agreement announcement declared the picket line would continue, but only to organize non-union workers.

The tranquility did not last long. Shortly thereafter, the Corrado Brothers, another Merchandise Mart sub-contractor, sued the Council in the Court of Chancery. They sought $50,000 for the delay-induced losses, citing the protest's "irreparable damage." Corrado Brothers denied in an official press release that there was "a bonafide labor dispute between their suppliers and their employees over wages, hours, or conditions of work."

Legal proceedings took a roundabout turn in December 1951 when the BTC tried to move the lawsuit to federal court. U.S. District Court Chief Judge Paul Leahy, however, remanded the case back to the state level.

Frustrated by court delays, the Corrado Brothers sought a restraining order against the picketing. Delaware Chancery Court Chancellor Collins J. Seitz refused to issue the order. He referenced the National Labor Relations Board (NLRB) citation that the Taft-Hartley Act legalized picket lines to solicit union membership.

Chancellor Seitz finally dismissed the Corrado Brothers' lawsuit. He invoked his court's lack of jurisdiction over interstate commerce disputes, which instead fell under the NLRB. Seitz reiterated an earlier position, ending the drawn-out legal struggle with a union victory for John S. Turulski in May 1952. *Merchandise Mart aerial: Delaware Public Archives/Glenn Rude Photo Collection/Action Photo Studios, Inc.*

Page 50 Space Suits

NASA sub-contractor ILC Industries carried the responsibility for the astronauts' lives. "Each Apollo suit was designed to sustain life while allowing mobility," said Tom Barr of ILC manufacturing. "The suits needed to be easy to put on, lightweight, convenient to store, and extremely reliable."

Founded in 1941 as International Latex Corporation, ILC initially focused on World War II military products, including life vests, rafts, and anti-exposure clothing. A 1947 expansion resulted in four divisions: Metals, Playtex, Chemical, and Pharmaceuticals.

The Navy and Air Force in 1952 contracted the Dover Metals Division to supply special high-altitude helmets. Several years later, the unit began providing pressurized flight suits as well. This experience laid the groundwork for ILC's critical role in space exploration, culminating in 1962 when the company began developing the Apollo spacesuit.

Each was custom-tailored to a specific astronaut and hand sewn. The three-man Apollo crew required nine suits per mission. Playtex seamstresses transitioned to the Metals Division, bringing skills in integrating soft goods with hard surfaces. This expertise, initially applied to women's undergarment girdle clasps, eventually played a crucial role in connecting spacesuit fasteners.

ILC had to make body plaster casts and measure each astronaut. Once the suit had been cut and stitched, ILC had to coax the astronaut back to Dover for a fit check. Design changes might have been needed due to such things as weight fluctuations.

The NASA contract led to major ILC organizational developments. Three years later, the newly formed Government and Industrial Division became the sole NASA spacesuit contractor, expanding to 200 workers.

"In the Apollo spacecraft, all the astronauts sat close together," said James Clougherty, an ILC Dover program manager. "The suits now had to be flexible, so they wouldn't keep banging into each other." The company solved the problem by pioneering "jointed-suit" technology. Such fabric molding techniques reduced bulky seams and made the joints more flexible.

ILC Dover built a plant in the nearby town of Frederica during the mid-1960s. This aerospace textile hub pioneered the innovative Beta Cloth. The material, woven from ultrafine glass fibers, offers high resistance to space's extreme temperatures and radiation. The Frederica and Dover facilities, working in tandem, synthesized the Apollo spacesuit, a technological marvel that had to operate flawlessly in the unyielding cosmos.

The imminent 1969 moon landing acted as a powerful incentive, leading ILC to intensify efforts to meet the Apollo program's ambitious objectives. The company's stringent quality measures, guiding the process from initial sketches to the final product, underscored their dedication. Their spacesuits went on to weather 250 flights, 6 moon landings, and over 3,000 hours of spacewalks. All took place without a single failure, testaments to mastery over materials, engineering, and quality control.

Neil Armstrong and Buzz Aldrin were the first of 12 Apollo astronauts to survive a lunar environment. On early flights, there was no guarantee the spacesuits would work as advertised. In hindsight, Americans can appreciate that the mission ran smoothly. However, Armstrong and Aldrin, together with their crewmate Mike Collins—who remained aboard the command module in lunar orbit—knew they were venturing into uncharted territory. The venture was fraught with potential dangers that were both physical and psychological. The astronauts, trained to maintain composure and focus on their tasks, were human nonetheless. They grappled with a mix of awe, fear, and a profound sense of isolation from being so far from loved ones.

Aldrin disclosed to *Life* magazine that he privately celebrated communion while the Apollo 11 lunar module rested on the moon's surface. He said he had stowed bread and wine aboard the ship and partook of it "just after Mike had passed over us one revolution, and we knew we were going to be on the moon for a while."

"I find it difficult to believe," Neil Armstrong later told reporters, "anyone could see the sights I was privileged to see and the views I was shown on my travel, and not be most aware of the power of the Supreme Being and His artwork."

ILC's technologies played a crucial role in enabling astronauts to witness celestial wonders. ILC spacesuits traveled on every manned Apollo mission, from 11 to 17. "Our suits were up there, and they did their job well," said spokesman Bruce Ferguson.

The once modest latex manufacturer experienced a remarkable ascent, becoming NASA's exclusive spacesuit contractor. ILC secured a place in history when Neil Armstrong took his "giant leap for mankind." *Spacesuit schematic public domain/NASA; ILC Dover photo courtesy ILC Dover Aerospace Technologies Archives*

Page 51 Beach Culture

Elvis Presley's groundbreaking musical explosion flared onto the world stage with 1954's "That's All Right." Two decades later, Delaware's own George Thorogood and the Destroyers took up the high-energy boogie blues style, echoing Elvis. Beach party culture—*Can you dig it, Daddio?*—integrated their infectious rhythms into a revolution of leisure, nightlife, and cultural expression.

Playboy magazine's devil-may-care premise took tangible expression in Delaware's unfolding beach scene. Launching in 1953, the publication glamorously depicted sexual liberation as an appealing alternative to the more conventional post-war lifestyle.

"We enjoy mixing up cocktails and an hors d'oeuvre or two," explained publisher Hugh Hefner, "putting a little mood music on the phonograph, and inviting in a female acquaintance for a quiet discussion on Picasso, Nietzsche, jazz, sex." Hefner's ethos came alive against a backdrop of rhythmic ocean waves.

Bygone times gave way to waterfronts now humming with the beatniks' growing rebellious spirit. "A beatnik," quipped *Morning News* columnist Earl Wilson, "is someone who has eliminated the job but kept the coffee break."

Society recognized the beach bums by their scruffy beards and French berets. These frequent coffee house habitués lived in grimy clothes. Often, they carried beat-up knapsacks filled with bongos. Many were avid readers of Jack Kerouac's *On the Road*. Their passed-around copies became noticeably well-worn.

The beatniks rejected the concept of the "organizational man" and instead sought spontaneous and authentic experiences. This approach was not universally accepted. Ocean City, Maryland, for example, took swift action in 1959 against a venture known as the Beatnik Club. City officials shut them down, citing neighborhood disturbance caused by lewd and raucous patrons. Nevertheless, Beat culture resonated in the live-and-let-live seaside corners of Bethany, Dewey, and Rehoboth.

Sussex County's picture postcard coastline towns started to build iconic coffee houses and nightclubs in the early 1960s. A decade or two later, the three beach locales evolved into a vibrant late-night scene attracting revelers from far and wide.

The proliferation of fast-food chains added another component to this paradigm shift. Mid-Atlantic companies such as Royal Farms and Wawa responded to the influx of beachgoers. They carved out competing niches to swiftly serve hungry travelers and their refueling needs. Grotto Pizza of Rehoboth Beach (est. 1960) expanded on a discovery made by Thrasher's French Fries decades earlier: boardwalk strollers did not require a sit-down restaurant. They were happy to eat in transit.

These cultural, culinary, and lifestyle transitions spurred significant infrastructure developments. The ferry from Cape May, New Jersey to Lewes launched in 1963. This Delaware Bay crossing improved Garden State residents' access to the First State's beaches. The water taxi offered an escape from "the grey flannel suit." Meanwhile, the Chesapeake Bay Bridge, built 11 years earlier, funneled Maryland's western shore vacationers onto U.S. Route 50, and thence to longed-for Sussex County beach refreshments.

Delaware's Department of Transportation initiated long-range planning for a segment of U.S. Route 1. They envisioned streamlining regional travel further by creating a direct connection from the Philadelphia area to in-state beaches. But that decades-long project would not be completed for another generation.

The societal shakeups of the 1950s and early 1960s were more than a fleeting phase. They built the engine that drove Sussex County's hospitality boom. By century's end, the state's southern dune-backed beaches accelerated into flourishing vacation hotspots.

Page 52 Delaware State Parks

First, the influx of federal funds drove the growth of Delaware's state parks, chiefly from the Land and Water Conservation Fund State Assistance Program. This 1965 legislation offered matching grants to states encouraging the acquisition and development of public outdoor recreation sites and facilities. These funds could also be funneled through states to assist local governments.

Peter Geldof, Jr., superintendent of Delaware State Parks at the time, had followed the path of the program from the time Congress introduced the bill in late 1962. He outlined a plan to the Delaware Assembly the following year to invest the expected funding should the federal bill be passed. Thanks to Geldof's advance planning and the bill's passage, Delaware established the new Cape Henlopen State Park in 1964, the state's largest, and one of the earliest, beneficiaries of such funding.

Second, members of wealthy families, on inheriting ancestral mansions, sometimes found themselves uninterested in maintaining large estates. Tax donation allowances presented an attractive solution: transfer ownership to the state.

Delaware consequently gained four magnificent state parks, each with unique historical flavor: Bellevue State Park, a legacy of William du Pont, Jr.; Auburn Valley State Park, former property of the Marshall dynasty; Alapocas Run State Park, which once housed the Joseph Bancroft Mills; and Brandywine Creek State Park, previously a du Pont family parcel.

Lastly, the 1960s surge in state park expansions was fueled by the federal government's disposition towards shedding properties no longer deemed necessary. This strategy resulted in the birth of five more state parks—Cape Henlopen, once a military base known as Fort Miles during World War II; Fort Delaware, home to the Union fortress of Civil War fame; Fort DuPont, named after the military facility housed there in the nineteenth and twentieth centuries; Fenwick Island, a barrier island utilized for coastal defense during World War II; and Delaware Seashore, once the site of the Indian River Inlet Station.

Certain properties, like Lums Pond and Killens Pond, transitioned into state parks due to diminished commercial value. Lums Pond, originally built in the early nineteenth century as a Chesapeake and Delaware Canal impoundment, found a new life as a state park in 1963. Similarly, the state acquired Killens Pond in 1965, a former millpond that had become an owner tax burden.

White Clay Creek State Park was born out of a struggle between public and private interests that began in the years following World War II. Responding to the threat of water shortages in northern Delaware after the war, DuPont Corporation quickly acquired lands surrounding White Clay Creek to propose creating a reservoir on the creek. This strategic initiative aimed to secure a consistent water supply during dry periods by harnessing the creek's flow. DuPont's heavy reliance on water for extensive industrial and chemical production activities drove the move.

Water played a critical role in facilitating chemical reactions, product testing, managing machinery-generated heat, and ensuring environmentally responsible waste treatment at DuPont's facilities. The proposed reservoir was thus seen as essential for maintaining a reliable water source to support these operations.

However, DuPont's plan soon faced fierce opposition from local citizens and groups such as the United Automobile Workers and the Sierra Club. The White Clay Watershed Association coalesced in 1965 against building the dam. The association opposed the plans due to environmental, recreational, water quality, and cultural concerns.

They argued that the project would destroy the creek's natural ecosystem, restrict access to outdoor activities, degrade local water quality, and threaten historic sites. Instead, the association advocated for alternative solutions like water conservation and infrastructure improvements to meet the region's water needs without compromising the creek's integrity.

A stalemate between environmentalists and business interests unfolded. DuPont abandoned their plans for the dam, yielding to environmental apprehensions and public outcry. The state acquired the land in 1968 and officially inaugurated White Clay Creek State Park before the end of the year.

Delaware's expansion of state parks in the 1960s was part of a larger national trend. The post-World War II period saw rapid urban growth and industrialization, leading to increased recognition of the need to preserve natural spaces. This era also marked the advent of the modern environmental movement, inspired by Rachel Carson's seminal 1962 work, *Silent Spring*.

Local evolution within Delaware's borders was a microcosm of the push for public spaces. Americans seeking to reconnect with nature had more disposable income and leisure time than prior generations. And so, a surge in hiking, fishing, boating, and camping led to expanded park creation as well. All told, these trends profoundly shaped Delaware's state park system, creating a future for all to enjoy. *Both photos: Delaware State Parks collection*

Page 53 Civil Rights Act

"I had to take a position on that," he said, "and I had to go up and down the state, because I knew people felt differently than I did, and I wanted them to understand all the aspects of [integration] as I saw it. I felt close to the people, I needed the benefit of their counsel and advice, and I wanted them to understand how I thought about it."

His efforts saved Delaware State College, founded in 1891 as the "State College for Colored Students," from fiscal ruin. "Delaware State College," he said in 1957, "has always amazed me with its vitality in spite of the years of neglect and the strife within its walls. The potential of the college has always been great, and it was decided that Delaware State College would either be a first-class college or none at all. I don't think there's any place for an inferior institution." Years later, Delaware State returned the favor by bestowing upon Boggs an honorary doctorate.

Delawareans elected Boggs to the U.S. Senate in 1960. Four years into his first term, he endorsed the proposed Civil Rights bill working through Congress. His keen understanding of the legislation's intricacies guided him in supporting key amendments.

Forty-five Delaware civil rights leaders went to Washington in April 1964 to meet with their senators, Boggs and John J. Williams. NAACP members, plus black and white clergymen, were part of the conclave. "Cale was our friend, and one of my favorite persons," said NAACP's Delaware branch president Littleton P. Mitchell. The visitors applauded Boggs, but not Williams, as the two entered the room. Boggs showed warm receptiveness to the movement and demonstrated his depth of commitment to the cause by promising to vote for the bill, provided certain conditions were met.

Boggs, always a moderate, supported two liberal addendums and an additional conservative two. Boggs advocated for progressive elements by resisting the removal of federal grants for teacher training in schools seeking desegregation. He also fought the exemption of smaller businesses from workplace discrimination.

However, he simultaneously supported conservative aspects of the bill such as the Mansfield-Dirksen Amendment, which curtailed the federal government's enforcement. Additionally, he advocated for increasing the authority of the Civil Rights Commission. "While I may not concur with every provision," Boggs reflected, "the essence of the Act is vital for the progress of our nation."

Born in Cheswold in 1909, Boggs graduated from Dover High School and the University of Delaware. He joined the Delaware National Guard in 1926, where he became a reserve officer, skillfully balancing academics with athletics and ROTC leadership. Boggs earned his law degree from Georgetown University in 1937 and worked for Logan and Duffy, a Wilmington law practice. He was called up from the reserves for active military duty in 1941.

His World War II service profoundly shaped his views on equality. Exposure to diverse soldiers and the injustices of a segregated military likely heightened his awareness of racial disparities. The shared sacrifices and camaraderie with troops of all races emphasized the irrationality of discrimination, contrasting sharply with the ideals of freedom and democracy he fought for.

As a Lieutenant Colonel, his leadership role underscored the importance of fairness and justice, influencing his civil rights stance in his later political career. Boggs earned the rank of Lieutenant Colonel in the 6th Armored Cavalry, 3rd U.S. Army, and was decorated for his actions under General Patton in the European theater.

Boggs launched his political career with election to the U.S. House of Representatives, serving there from 1946-1953, then becoming Delaware governor. J. Caleb Boggs' extensive experience, from his Delaware roots to the Senate corridors, placed him at the forefront of improving the lives of all Americans. This political centrist emerged as an unlikely champion of one of U.S. history's most radical legislative acts. His ability to navigate opposition and build new coalitions proved crucial to the Civil Rights Act.

The State of Delaware constructed the Caleb Boggs Federal Building in Wilmington two years after the Civil Rights Act became law, named in recognition of the senator's contributions. "The best way for me to sum up Cale was that he didn't live a lie," said then-Senator Joe Biden years later at Bogg's 1993 funeral. "Most politicians, after they leave public office, it's the last time you see them at a fund-raising dinner for the poor. Cale Boggs did everything that he did while a senator, after he was a senator."

The landmark 1964 legislation finally extended long-denied protections and opportunities to black Americans. Senator Boggs' centrist leadership and conviction helped pave the way for hard-won victories. Ending segregation and inequality would require tireless activism. Nonetheless, the Civil Rights Act enshrined in law new beginnings for justice. *Photo Caesar Rodney High School students playing ball: Delaware Public Archives; photo Caleb Boggs with airman and plane: collection 166th Airlift Wing Public Affairs/Delaware Air National Guard*

Page 54 First Community College

The SEED program's ethos is part of the broader American community college movement, initiated in the early twentieth century. This endeavor, appreciably influenced by Dr. William Rainey Harper, aimed to make local post-secondary education more accessible. His contributions culminated in creating the first junior college in 1901. So began a trend that redefined the first two years of college as a steppingstone to the traditional four-year school.

Over the decades, the perception and role of junior colleges evolved, shifting from being seen merely as extensions of high school education to becoming recognized as vital institutions in their own right.

Across the country, states rapidly established community college networks. However, the growth was uneven, influenced by geography, politics, and demographics. States like California, Texas and Illinois built dozens of community colleges by the 1940s. But their vast size posed challenges. In Texas, for example, some residents face 170-mile drives to attend the nearest community college. This contrasts sharply with tiny Delaware, whose geography ensures college accessibility for every resident.

In the early to mid-twentieth century, Delaware's economy was heavily influenced by companies like DuPont, which enabled many residents to earn middle-class salaries without a college degree. This culture of promotion from within offered a viable pathway to upward mobility, with hands-on experience often compensating for the lack of academic schooling.

However, as the economic landscape evolved and the demand for qualifications increased, the role of such companies in providing attainable career advancement began to diminish. This shift highlighted the growing importance of formal education and set the stage for the emergence of community colleges to bridge the gap.

Many students appeared content with the educational opportunities at regional and out-of-state four-year institutions. Alternatively, they might have considered technical apprenticeships, like those offered by Wilmington's Goldey Beacom School of Business. Teacher's colleges, like vocational schools, were primarily concerned with preparing students for a specific career. Delaware State University, for example, originated for that purpose. However, these options were not always accessible or affordable for all students. This situation highlighted the need for more local and cost-effective alternatives.

The wider recognition of community colleges' importance led to concerns among some in academia. G. Bruce Dearing, the Dean of the University of Delaware, was one such educator. He voiced his fear, in October 1961, that redirecting tax dollars to these new institutions could cut into the funding for existing universities.

His remarks highlighted Delaware's budget constraints, stalling momentum for establishing community colleges. These fiscal challenges needed to be addressed before the eventual founding of Delaware Technical and Community College (DTCC).

E. Hall Downes, first president of DTCC's board of trustees, voiced frustration over public skepticism towards community colleges. "One of our biggest problems ... is the fact that parents do not appreciate what technical and vocational training means. The only thing that has any prestige with them is the four-year college."

Despite these local concerns and challenges, President Lyndon Johnson's Higher Education Facilities Act brought Delaware schools

110

to the brink of change. This December 1963 legislation committed $1 billion in federal aid over three years to invest in postsecondary academic centers of learning.

The bill also mandated that each state allocate 22 percent of these funds specifically to public two-year community colleges and technical institutes. The policy shift also played a key role in encouraging states, including Delaware, to invest more heavily in local and affordable higher education options.

Delaware positioned itself to take action, with the Higher Education Facilities Act paving the way for increased investment in community colleges. Spurred by the promise of federal funding, the Delaware General Assembly acted at last (—only 65 years after America's very first community college had been founded.) Within three years of Johnson's initiative, state lawmakers founded the Delaware Technical and Community College (also DTCC or Del Tech). The Assembly laid the groundwork for an umbrella system consisting of four campuses.

The state strategically leveraged existing resources to establish the school's campuses as the network began to take shape. The legislature established DTCC Georgetown in the former William C. Jason High School, named after Delaware State College's first African American president.

The college listed two major education programs: one to qualify students for semiprofessional employment, and a 2-year college transfer program. Support included guidance counseling and remedial education services. Del Tech actively pursued cooperative planning with external stakeholders, spanning industry, various professions, government agencies, and the local community. The second-year enrollment doubled. This expansion necessitated construction to accommodate more laboratories and classrooms.

DTCC continued to grow and evolve over the following decades, establishing itself as a key player in Delaware's higher education landscape. "Delaware Tech has been a leader in technology training," summed up a *News Journal* editorial in late 1999. "Its work in this area has augmented the state's reputation as business friendly. The college's involvement in teaching General Motors workers new technology, for example, contributed to GM's decision to keep the Boxwood Road plant open in Newport. Now Delaware's secret is a national model. Del Tech has been named the 1999 Community College of the Year. It's a signal honor that should make all residents proud." Come 2000, over 12,000 students enrolled annually in DTCC courses and programs, evidence of the institution's impact in a mere few decades.

DTCC Georgetown is today nicknamed the "Southern Campus," otherwise called the Jack F. Owens campus. Three others are in place: Stanton Campus in Newark, the Charles L. Terry Campus in Dover, and the Orlando J. George, Jr. Campus in Wilmington.

The Delaware Technical Community College system embodies an early vision of advocates like William Rainey Harper, who aspired to create affordable, community-integrated ones. This reflects a broader movement towards democratizing higher education for all income levels. Beyond merely bridging the gap to four-year universities, these colleges have established themselves as key educational establishments. Over a quarter of Delaware's population had benefited from DTCC's offerings by the turn of the millennium. *Both exterior and classroom photos of school: Delaware Public Archives/Delaware Technical and Community College collection*

Page 55 Vocational Schools

The Marshallton Board of Education took notice of Bachman's innate leadership skills during her teacher's aide years. The members elected her chairperson in 1963, the first woman to hold the post.

What motivated Martha Bachman to transition from a teacher's aide to a leader? Her anger at politicians who were either indifferent or hostile to the nuanced learning needs of differently-abled children.

"Someday, very soon," she said in 1965, "we people in Delaware must decide whether our educational system is to be run by our professionals in the Department of Public Instruction, along with our State Board of Education, or by our General Assembly. If it is to be the latter, we are in for some real trouble."

The Delaware Advisory Council on Vocational Education (DACVE) in 1969 selected Bachman as their first chairperson. This state-level role, in turn, earned her national recognition. The following year, President Richard Nixon appointed Bachman as the first woman to serve on the National Advisory Council.

"The public schools are obligated," said the outspoken proponent, "either to prepare students to go on to higher education or to offer a curriculum that will insure them a secure job when they graduate."

Bachman played a critical role as DACVE chairperson. She used her own brand of leadership to shape the First State's policies, programs, and practices in career and technical education. "Most people feel a person isn't honorable unless he goes to college . . . The sooner we get out of the non-college bound label and into the career-oriented label, the better off we'll be," she said.

Martha Bachman was not one to mince words when addressing societal shortcomings. One 1974 letter to the *Evening Journal* castigated Delaware for lack of support for public education and cultural activities. "We have the second highest non-white public school population in the nation in the city of Wilmington.

"Yet, we turn our back on these schools and tell them to solve their own problems. We have a sorry record of increases in school funding being defeated at both the local district level and by our General Assembly. So, what is left to put in our brochure to sell Delaware as a wonderful place to work? And live? And play?"

Bachman received numerous distinctions and honors during her lifetime. However, for her, the real reward was the tangible change she could affect. "When you study something and know it thoroughly, people will start to listen to you," she observed.

Martha Bachman was the midwife to the birth of the New Castle County Vocational Technical School District. She did everything but hammer nails and run electrical wires to get Delcastle Technical High School built. "I believe that the thrust of vocational education should be to prepare our students to survive in a highly specialized and competitive job market," she insisted.

Bachman blended practicality with passion in private life as well. Always a "dirt gardener," she relished rolling up both sleeves. Her hands-on approach to new ground underscored a fierce determination: plant the seeds and then say, "Grow, darn you, grow."

Martha Bachman became one of the first Delawareans to win the Thomas Jefferson Award from the American Institute for Public Service. The prestigious recognition honors individuals for their outstanding public service, volunteerism, and efforts in community and social betterment. Jacqueline Kennedy Onassis, Senator Robert Taft Jr., and Sam Beard established the Jefferson Award in 1972.

Bachman passed away in 1998 at age 74. Those who knew her recognized a legacy that broadcast the seeds of reform, inclusion, and opportunity far and wide. *Watercolor by Theresa (Terre) Walton, for the Delaware Women's Hall of Fame; Delcastle Technical High School photo courtesy Delaware Public Archives*

Page 56 Bird Migration

Any decline of the region's indigenous and/or beneficial species could have adverse effects across the First State. For a host of reasons, the need for a sanctuary protecting the abundant migrating birds became readily apparent by the 1930s. The state's wealth of natural habitats helped foster a growing commitment to environmental stewardship. Bombay Hook National Wildlife Refuge, located nine miles southeast of Smyrna, marked a fresh chapter in the region's preservation.

Dedicated conservation efforts and support of federal legislation made the refuge's birth possible. Such a creation embodies a series of important steps to protect critical wetland habitats and the wildlife depending on them. Key pieces of legislation, i.e. the Migratory Bird Conservation Act and the Migratory Bird Hunting Stamp Act, played a crucial role in making this sanctuary a reality.

Hunters' duck license fees funded the 1937 federal government marshland purchase. This acquisition provided a year-round sanctuary for various waterfowl species, including mallards, black ducks, and pintails, as well as herons, owls, and white-tailed deer, ensuring the protection of these creatures and their habitats.

For wildlife, the haven's safeguarding represents a critical turning point. The state established estuary ecology and conservation-based priorities, placing them on equal footing with the needs of Delaware's agriculturally based land use.

Bombay Hook is primarily a tidal salt marshland. However, the refuge also encompasses 1,100 acres of impounded freshwater ponds, a result of meticulous wildlife management. These artificial catchments, built between 1939 and 1961, are intended to mimic natural avian habitats. The water levels change to match various seasonal transitions. The model ensures a hospitable environment for the survival of both wading birds and those seeking deeper channels.

Both local farmers and the refuge, together, benefit from ongoing cooperation. The planters get a tax break on adjacent land. In turn, they gladly share some of their post-harvest corn with the sanctuary's inhabitants.

The marshland's undisturbed ecosystem contributes vitally to the local fishing industry. It offers a natural reservoir where spawned fish can grow before venturing into open waters. Wetlands likewise provide nurseries for a myriad of other marine life.

Bombay Hook encompasses migratory as well as nesting bird populations. The Southern bald eagle, an endangered species, finds a home here. However, they struggle with reproduction. Park personnel each year barricade refuge roads within a half-mile radius of eagle nesting perches. The birds hover over their clutches well beyond the five-week incubation period. Still, their eggs never hatch.

The bald eagle's infertility issues at Bombay Hook were linked to the widespread use of DDT on area cropland from 1945 until its ban in 1972. The pesticide seeped into the marshes and contaminated the food chain. DDT accumulated in the fish consumed by eagles, leading to concentrated doses that disrupted the birds' calcium metabolism and resulted in thinner, more fragile eggshells.

Delaware has progressed through phases of industrialization and urbanization. This development has necessitated corresponding changes in environmental policies. Yet, Bombay Hook remains a living classroom for wildlife enthusiasts, courtesy of state and local preservationists. The migrating wildlife rests amidst the tranquility of nature's shielded sanctuary.

Some visitors drive the refuge's dirt roads flanking the pools' perimeters, drawn by the remoteness and delicate beauty. Others choose to stand by, immersing themselves in the serene respite's signature charm. Here, a mute swan, over there, a great blue heron.

The 'blues' walk against the current, seen as solitary sentinels gracing the skyline. Out on the ocean, thousands of Atlantic pintails gather to roost for the night. A flock of snow geese cuts sharply into the clouds. At day's end, dun-colored deer blend into the evening shadows of unique habitats that stretch for miles and miles across pristine Delaware coastline.

Delaware's unique geography along the Atlantic Flyway makes the state a critical stopover each year for countless migratory birds. Delmarva's diverse habitats are a vibrant testimony to the ever-evolving landscape of tidal marshes, freshwater ponds, and coastal wetlands. All-in-all, they provide essential resting and refueling points for birds navigating the long journey between spring breeding grounds in the north and over-wintering sites in the south. *Wildlife photo: Catoledo/Flickr*

Page 57 Delaware Wild Lands, Inc.

The newly minted man-about-town filled his days in Florida with loose living, playing the piano, singing, and fishing in the state's sun-kissed waters. Harvey eventually started his own resort, shuttling regularly between the family's Wilmington manse and the Keys.

Playboy fantasies, and living the alcohol-fueled high life, got the best of him. The turning point came when Harvey volunteered to work as a guide in the Florida Everglades, which had been ravaged by dredging and unregulated lumbering.

"My experience of what's happened to cypress in Florida—nearly total destruction—made me want not to see the same happen in Delaware," he said later. "Vast stands were annihilated." That shock galvanized him to do something socially meaningful. He sobered up at age 49, put the Florida party routine behind him, and turned his attention to the Delaware cypress groves which infatuated him as a boy. Harvey began to re-imagine his role in the world of wetland conservation with innovative seriousness. He left behind the frivolity of his youth and dedicated himself with renewed purpose to protecting his home state's fragile marshes. Passion turned to action. The once-aimless playboy had found his calling. Delaware's natural treasures would be the beneficiary.

This evolution led him back to Delaware for good. His sights were now set, and he was determined to make a difference. Tapping into du Pont family connections as powerful allies, he was able to assemble a team of nine Wilmington philanthropists of similar fervor and persuasion. They collaborated to establish Delaware Wild Lands, Inc. (DWL) in September 1961. Philadelphia Conservationists, Inc. underwrote an $8,000 loan to kickstart the new venture.

These network ties helped Harvey quickly build a nucleus of land purchases in the organization's nascent years. Edward and Viola Arvey, for example, sold DWL ten acres. An additional investor came forward and offered another 80 acres at Trussum Pond. Word spread fast and the parcel sizes grew in tandem. Sussex Trust Company in late 1962 conveyed the organization 119 acres.

The environmentalist's impact extended to the shore salt marshes alongside other efforts. The Ted Harvey Wildlife Area is adjacent to the 16,000-acre Bombay Hook National Wildlife Refuge. This proximity suggests a shared commitment to the protection of unique habitats for thousands of wetland species. Both visions aligned with an overlapping concern for disappearing soil resources, core breeding grounds of migratory birds, land-based waterfowl, and other associated wildlife.

In the winter 1963 issue of the *Delaware Conservationist* magazine, Harvey eloquently stated his dedication to expanding wilderness protection efforts. His article "Planning Isn't Dreaming" advocated for perpetuating the natural landscape of Cape Henlopen with area dunes, wind-twisted pines, and small hidden ponds. Harvey called for proactive programming to safeguard the shores along Rehoboth Bay, Indian River, and Assawoman Bay from future development. Just two years later, the *Delaware Conservationist* named him as their Man of the Year in recognition of his crucial environmental activism.

Harvey and his teammates reached a milestone in August 1964. They acquired a 1,200-acre tract within the Great Pocomoke Swamp. This much-sought triumph, Delaware Wild Lands' crown jewel, contained "fine, large specimens of the old-growth bald cypress." These swamp-loving trees survived centuries of lumbering, forest fires, and drainage. One of Harvey's most cherished landscapes is a world unto itself. Towering bald cypresses, their trunks adorned with shaggy, rust-colored bark, rise from the murky waters like ancient sentinels. The still waters mirror the lush canopy above, broken only by the occasional splash of a diving wood duck.

This rich tapestry of life extends to the shore salt marshes, where the rhythmic ebb and flow of tides nourishes a complex web of biodiversity. The slender, green blades of cordgrass sway in unison with the wind, while fiddler crabs scuttle across the muddy banks, their brilliant red claws a vibrant contrast to the muted hues. The air is filled with the trilling calls of red-winged blackbirds and the haunting cries of great blue herons, a symphony of sound that underscores the vital importance of these wetland habitats. "The conservation of the cypress swamp, along with Trussum Pond and the Delaware salt marshes, was one of the main reasons for organizing Delaware Wild Lands," Harvey proclaimed.

The local community reacted with surprise and delight at the acquisition of Pocomoke Swamp's vast wide-open space. "The purchase of land for preservation in its natural state has ... brought much delight among old timers," *News Journal* columnist Constance Brown remarked soon thereafter. "The rest of us are still somewhat stunned by the impact of something so wonderful happening right in our own backyard."

However, Harvey's deepening concern for the environment soon propelled him into direct confrontation with industrial threats to Delaware's natural landscapes. He feared the construction of a proposed Shell Oil refinery would ruin the beauty of the salt marshes along the southern New Castle County coast. Thus, in 1971, he raised $1 million to buy land surrounding Shell's intended site. This successful checkmate blocked access, aborting the company's plans.

Gov. Russell Peterson joined forces with Harvey to propose legislation limiting industrial development up and down the state's fragile coastal marshes. The fight led to the Coastal Zone Act (see page 58) passing that same year.

The conservationist took extraordinary pride in preserving 10,000 acres of the Great Cypress Swamp. This vulnerable landscape, stretching from Frankford to Gumboro, became known simply as the "Great Swamp." The habitat area bears witness to a vibrant history, including clandestine Prohibition-era bootlegging operations.

Ted Harvey foresaw the importance of creating numerous wilderness areas, recognizing their ongoing contribution to the quality of life. Furthermore, his impassioned insights galvanized, among others, the National Wildlife Federation, Delawareans for Orderly Development, and Ducks Unlimited, all of whom joined in promoting these noble regional efforts.

"Ted was truly an inspired and inspiring individual," recalled Lorraine Fleming, Delaware Nature Society's manager of conservation and preservation for 30-plus years. "He had a knack for clutching wild areas from the jaws of destructive development."

Edmund "Ted" Harvey's tireless dedication to preserving Delaware's natural treasures left an indelible mark on the state's environmental landscape. His visionary leadership, unwavering commitment to ecological protection, and instrumental role in the passage of the Coastal Zone Act continue to inspire and guide Delaware's conservation efforts today. *Everglade dredging and lumbering photos courtesy Florida Memory Project; Ted Harvey portrait courtesy Bruce Harvey via Findagrave.com; carpenter frog courtesy John Bunnell/ Virginia Department of Wildlife Resources; zebra swallowtail butterfly courtesy Megan McCarty/Wikipedia; prothonotary warbler courtesy Delaware Ornithological Society*

Page 58 Coastal Zone Act

Governor Peterson appealed to this group of discontented citizens, aiming to advance his own agenda. He argued for the necessity of a strong legal framework to ensure ongoing statewide environmental protection. Industries might exert undue influence over local zoning boards, potentially swaying decisions using under-the-table favors.

Peterson's fierce advocacy secured the bill's passage. The Delaware Department of Natural Resources and Environmental Control praised the measure's efficacy in safeguarding sensitive coastal areas. Furthermore, "...species diversity has shown a 20% increase since the Act's implementation," stated a paper from the University of Delaware's Environmental Research Division.

Critics found the Act overly restrictive. Skeptics targeted the now-or-never thinking of Peterson's supporters credited for the passage. Among these, the Delaware Tomorrow Commission (DTC) cited what they perceived as the governor's lack of logic.

Bernard Hessler, Jr., a Wilmington lawyer and DTC member, contended that advocates for the Coastal Zone Act were making broad, sweeping generalizations. He mocked their flawed reasoning that if some refineries pollute, then all of them are guilty and therefore should be banned. The Coastal Zone Act institutionalized anti-business policies, said Peterson's detractors.

The DTC commission assessed the law five years post-implementation and concluded that the initial Coastal Zone Act needed replacement. State Planner David Keifer in 1976 compiled a comprehensive statewide land-use planning act to propose to Governor Sherman W. Tribbitt as a substitute, who shared the draft with the DTC. The group attended hearings to review the suggestions before Keifer sent them to the General Assembly.

Russell Peterson, now serving as an 'amicus curiae,' along with his original supporters, insisted that the law must remain as is. They aimed to ward off "polluting industries waiting for an opportune moment to enter Delaware."

The General Assembly declared in the end that the Coastal Zone Act did not "contravene the existing authorities of counties and local governments with respect to planning." The Delaware Tomorrow Commission's proposed changes went nowhere. In fact, the law stood as originally framed for 46 years. The act's original intention—preserving Delaware's coastline—appears to have been met. But questions about unintended consequences have arisen.

Critics argue the Act hinders the state's economic growth. Nevertheless, there is no such conclusive evidence. "In the long run," observed *News Journal* columnist Ralph Moyed in 2000, "Delaware's action to protect the Coastal Zone seems to have had no liability and sometimes is an asset in efforts — largely successful — to attract 'the right kind' of industry to Delaware."

The Act's banning of specific industries—steel and paper mills, petrochemical complexes, and oil refineries—remains a point of tension. Critics question whether these blanket prohibitions are the most effective or fair means of environmental protection. They argue that the law, without ongoing revisions, might not adapt well to new economic and ecological realities.

The Coastal Zone Act highlights the underlying competition between current environmental preservation and future business interests. Even today, continual debates arise over job issues vs. industrial restrictions.

Page 59 Women's Rights Commission

Friedan identified the widespread malaise among housewives as "the problem that has no name" and argued that women were being denied the opportunity to reach their full potential due to systemic barriers and discrimination.

President John F. Kennedy made parity a part of his agenda. Early in his tenure, JFK assembled the first-ever national Commission on the Status of Women. The group's implementation reinvigorated support for the Equal Rights Amendment, first introduced in 1923, which aimed to guarantee equitable legal status for all women.

Inspired by the President's Commission on the Status of Women, Rosella Humes, president of Delaware's Professional Women's Society, collaborated with in-state leaders Wilhemina Miller and Grace Stirba. They proposed a Delaware commission to Governor Elbert Carvel (1961-5), who immediately appointed them. The Governor's Commission on the Status of Women (GCSW) channeled feminist ideologies into actionable policy recommendations starting in 1963.

"We do not face some of the obvious problems of women in other states," Humes commented at the GCSW's first organization meeting. "There is no reason why we should set out to prove that the women of Delaware are downtrodden and neglected. Instead, we will make every effort to find out precisely how women are treated in Delaware.

"My feeling is that for too long the abilities of qualified women in regard to policy making and jobs in the higher echelons have been ignored," said Humes. "I would be the first one to not be satisfied if a woman were appointed just because she was a woman. It's a case again of accepting individuals on their own talents."

Humes, Miller, and Stirba convinced Governor Carvel to launch a task force in November 1963, focusing on gender inequalities in both homes and professional life. He selected 17 other prominent constituents in education, government, the press, law, and labor. The commission's subcommittees offered a range of recommendations, covering everything from labor laws to income tax reforms. The resulting 37-page report, "Delaware's Women Today (1964)," aimed to shape state policies regarding women.

The following year, the Delaware Federation of Business and Professional Women took a leading role in advocating for the repeal of "protective" labor laws. These 52-year-old statutes imposed restrictions on female employees' workforce participation. They specifically limited work hours, prohibited night work, barred entry into certain industries, and mandated explicit working conditions.

The lobbying worked. When Charles Terry succeeded Carvel as governor, he guided House Bill 382 through the legislative process to passage in December 1965. The bill simply read that "the female labor laws of Delaware are repealed." This action captured national attention and established a model that various other states in the U.S. would later consider for their own legislative approaches.

GCSW's early support for the Equal Rights Amendment proved prescient. Delaware became the second state in March 1972 to ratify it. This endorsement symbolized a major step for female equality and fortified the state's reputation as a pioneer in women's rights.

However, the battle was far from over. A mere five months after this historic ratification, Norma B. Handloff, an original member of the Governor's Commission on the Status of Women and then-mayor of Newark, addressed a crowd in Wilmington commemorating the passage of the 19th Amendment.

Despite the recent ERA victory, Handloff emphasized the persistent inequalities women still faced, citing the wage gap, higher unemployment rates, and the undervaluing of housewives' work in the Social Security system. She lashed out at the retirement structure that gave housewives less than $2,000 a year because "their pension is based on earned income, and their work as housewives has not 'earned' them anything." Handloff urged more women and men who supported gender equality to seek positions of authority, stressing that the fight against sexual discrimination was "a job that needs doing."

Delaware's early ratification of the ERA was a worthy milestone. However, Handloff's impassioned speech, coming so closely on the heels of this achievement, provided a poignant reminder that true equality remained an ongoing struggle. The First State had taken a crucial step forward, but the journey towards women's rights was far from complete.

Page 60 Arts Council

Their fiery exchanges over federal funding reflected wider national debates on the arts' best use of such support. These discussions had gained momentum since the National Endowment for the Arts appeared on the scene in 1965. During this period, Evan Turner served as the director of the Philadelphia Museum of Art. In a 1969 editorial, he praised the creation of the Delaware State Arts Council. His sentiments echoed those of President Lyndon Johnson, who said "Art is a nation's most precious heritage. Our works of art reveal to ourselves and to others the inner vision which guides us as a nation. And where there is no vision, the people perish."

Amid the optimism about arts funding, the disagreement between Craig Gilborn and Otto Dekom was to be expected. Rather than indicating systemic failure, their conflict highlighted the complexities of turning ambitious goals into action.

Gilborn had served as program administrator of the Virginia Museum of Fine Arts in Richmond for three years. This was followed by five years as an associate in Winterthur Museum's education division before joining the Delaware Arts Council. He had been an adjunct instructor at the University of Delaware, having earned his master's degree in arts from the Winterthur program in early American culture. Taking the helm as the Arts Council's first executive director, Gilborn sought to prioritize native talent. He declared that local artists constituted the "bedrock of any thriving arts scene."

At the same time, Otto Dekom, a complex multifaceted figure, held a unique position in Wilmington's cultural landscape. "The man Delawareans loved to hate" combined roles as a music critic and public relations professional with a background in economics and politics. His reputation for intellectual rigor was matched by participation in the local theater scene, both as an actor and a dialogue coach. By 1962, Dekom had become Delaware's premier theater critic, a position that augmented his arts community influence. When he and Gilborn finally crossed paths, Dekom minced no words. "The new Arts Council chair has put a ceiling on our cultural future by favoring local amateur groups over professional ones."

Differences in age and upbringing colored the perspectives of both men. Michigan native Gilborn, at 34, was navigating the early stages of his career, while Dekom, 51, had strong classicist views stemming from his native Romanian heritage.

Their ideologies clashed in a very public manner. Dekom accused Gilborn of fostering a provincial mindset, of being content with cultural mediocrity, citing the Council's funding of amateur jazz concerts over professional orchestras.

Dekom's scathing criticisms echoed cultural elites across the country. They feared local focus would undermine artistic excellence.

News Journal columnist Bill Frank defended Dekom, emphasizing the constructive nature of his reviews. Gilborn, for his part, highlighted the Council's financial struggles, exacerbated by inadequate support from the Delaware state legislature. In the year 1970-71, for example, the Council received a modest appropriation of just $50,000.

Despite these constraints, Gilborn and the Council explored a range of initiatives to support Delaware arts. These included conducting a major conference on the arts, offering matching grants to local orchestras in Newark and Dover, supplying discounted tickets for young people to attend performing arts events, and funding visiting theater groups to perform works such as *Hamlet*. The Council also considered creating an artsmobile for traveling exhibits and establishing a new community theater group in Milford.

Gilborn championed local talent, asserting, "The Council's role extends beyond merely promoting established excellence." He dismissed expectations of an instant cultural renaissance as naïve. Gilborn saw Delaware as a hub for grassroots development, while Dekom preferred importing established works and artists.

Dekom denounced Gilborn's hesitance to invite professional musicians, suggesting in the *News Journal* that this approach leaves Delaware "in the backwash of the great cultural wave." He expressed disappointment that the Arts Council had not made significant artistic contributions, despite having already spent a large portion of its budget.

Otto Dekom continued his unrelenting scrutiny of Gilborn's tenure. In an October 1971 *Morning News* column, Dekom lambasted the cancellation of the customary pre-concert cocktail party and dinner held before Delaware Symphony concerts.

Dekom set Gilborn in stark contrast to previous speakers, such as William Smith, the assistant conductor of the Philadelphia Orchestra, and Michael Straight, an author and former editor of *The New Republic*. He praised these earlier speakers for their oratory prowess. Meanwhile, he bluntly stated that Gilborn — "whatever his erudition — is not a great speaker."

Dekom further argued that Gilborn's planned appearance led to the disappointing attendance numbers and eventual cancellation of the event. The council, under Gilborn, had supported the Delaware Symphony for two consecutive seasons, but Dekom implied that Gilborn's lack of public speaking skill could undermine even financial contributions.

Craig Gilborn lasted three years in the hot seat. In June 1972 he headed to Blue Mountain Lake, New York to become director of the Adirondack Museum, where he finished out his career. But not before being feted with a gracious Gala Evening hosted by the Delaware Art Museum. At this event, 15 of the state's cultural institutions thanked him for his contributions. "The magnitude of the party caught the Gilborns by surprise," reported the *News Journal*.

The former executive director's exit interview in that newspaper a few days later brought closure to his and Dekom's public spat. He chose not to engage directly with the latter's criticisms, a dignified silence that spoke volumes.

Instead, Craig Gilborn left with a call to action for increased public and corporate support for the arts. "The once-popular notion that wealthy benefactors could single-handedly sustain the arts in Delaware has faded into myth," he said. Gilborn suggested that the Delaware State Arts Council should consider branching into environmental issues, touching on topics like billboards and high-rise power lines that affect the state's aesthetics. Otto Dekom continued at the *Morning News* until his 1983 retirement, transitioning to food criticism from 1972 onwards.

The vitriol between Gilborn and Dekom, while reflective of their convictions, underscores the Gordian knot dilemmas in federal arts funding. This historical episode in Delaware's arts community, marked by passionate debate and contrasting philosophies, represented a microcosm of national dynamics. The feud highlighted the necessity of balancing local talent cultivation with the introduction of renowned artistic works. Arts communities nationwide are forever forced to make such intricate tightrope-walking decisions.
photo of Punch puppet courtesy Victoria and Albert Museum, London

Page 61 Gore-Tex Invented

"He definitely believed it would succeed, and my mother had great faith in him." The elder Gore was not afraid of failure. "His saying was 'jump in the water and see if you can swim.' His attitude was 'don't spend too much time preparing for something. Go do it.'"

Gore & Associates unexpectedly birthed their most renowned product, Gore-Tex, in 1969. This revolutionary material originated from the Gores' innovative work on computer ribbon cables. The manufacturing process utilized a compound known as polytetrafluoroethylene (PTFE), more commonly known to cooks as Teflon.

Roy Plunkett, a chemist at DuPont, discovered Teflon by accident when a gas he was experimenting with unexpectedly turned into a slippery, white solid instead of behaving as he anticipated. This 1938 discovery would later pave the way for a DuPont spin-off, Chemours, to take on the Teflon manufacturing mantle.

Fast forward three decades to W.L. Gore & Associates, and we find Bob Gore, immersed in his own world of invention, wrestling with the challenge of producing plumber's tape from PTFE more efficiently.

He grappled with a fabrication method that was not just costly but also clunky and time-consuming. This traditional process involved slowly stretching heated PTFE rods, a method Gore found inefficient. He abruptly yanked a heated PTFE rod in a moment of frustration, leading to an unexpected breakthrough.

The rapid stretching caused the polymer to expand by 800 percent, forming a lightweight, microporous structure composed of about 70 percent air. This new form of PTFE, surprisingly, was not only porous but also waterproof. "We knew we had something," said Gore. Gore dubbed this nonflammable, tough, waxy, and strong synthetic resin ePTFE (expanded polytetrafluoroethylene).

W. L. Gore & Associates introduced an initial use of ePTFE in 1970, aimed at their high-speed coaxial cable base. However, the company later identified a more substantial application in the textile industry. Gore discovered bonding ePTFE to fabric resulted in a material able to repel water. The fusing allowed perspiration vapor to permeate, providing an optimal balance of protection and breathability. This lamination could be tailored to create a lightweight, versatile, all-weather waterproof layer.

Capitalizing on this breakthrough, Gore made his first commercial sale in 1976. Early Winters, Ltd., a Seattle-based outdoor clothing company, became the first to purchase the newly created Gore-Tex. The world of moisture-proof textiles changed forever.

Gore & Associates engaged in a complex legal battle in the early 1980s, filing a lawsuit against Garlock, Inc. for using Gore's patented ePTFE process. The dispute centered around Garlock's use of a machine bought from John W. Cropper, a New Zealand engineer who had independently discovered ePTFE but failed to patent his process. Despite the intricacies of the case, involving questions of patent rights and the timing of Cropper's discovery, the Delaware court ultimately upheld the validity of W. L. Gore's patent.

The company went on to specialize in fluoropolymer-derived products under Bob Gore's helm, later growing into a multinational manufacturing enterprise. Their portfolio eventually encompassed a wide range of consumer and industrial products. Synthetic resin development continued to drive changes across a broad spectrum of industries, including oil & gas, chemicals, medical equipment, space industry, and electronics.

The firm became a billion-dollar enterprise during Bob Gore's tenure as president. Marking the occasion in 1996, Gore said, "We plan to leave a legacy to society and to future generations: infants with surgically reconstructed hearts that live because of our medical products; governments of free societies that are better able to protect themselves because of defense products; communities with cleaner and healthier environments because of our filtration and sealant products. And yes, people that just have more fun in the outdoors because of our Gore-Tex outerwear."

The story of Gore-Tex, emerging in the 1960s, exemplifies the unpredictable nature of revolutionary advancements. Such ground-breakers highlight the role of serendipity and exploration in science, transcending mere fabric development. Gore-Tex's evolution from an accidental discovery to a staple in various industries embodies the surprising and unexpected pathways of trailblazing inventions. *Swatch photo courtesy W. L. Gore & Associates, Inc.*

Page 62 Low-number License Plates

Animated auctioneers, the unique cadence of their theatrics echoing a rhythmic patois, fetch six-figure sums from the highest bidders. Gifted hawkers, their tongues spinning like helicopter blades, expertly push prices to impressive heights. Buyers, recognizing the deep-rooted status these plates confer, willingly engage in fierce bidding wars.

The auction hall buzzes with motorists' desire as they bid for these coveted numbers. Every shout from a sweat-slicked auctioneer sends waves of anticipation crashing through the crowd. Hands shoot up like desperate flags in the storm of competing bids. Each successful purchase is a thunderclap, a triumphant roar that mingles with the heady scent of victory and the bitter tang of defeat. "You look at the prices over time, it's a good investment—probably a lot better than the stock market," says savvy gavel master K. Wade Wilson of Lincoln, a University of Delaware business graduate.

Are low number plates only desirable in Delaware? Only lately? No, and no. On January 4, 1936, a Lynn, Massachusetts motorist sought state supreme court action to restore to him a low-number license plate he had held for six years but let lapse. The registrar instead offered Nicholas Mathey registration 36518. He flatly refused.

One might think the fascination with low-numbers would predominantly occur in smaller states. Delaware, after all, is the second smallest state and Massachusetts the sixth smallest. The value of such tags in close-knit communities is magnified because locals, more often than not, know their neighbors. In larger states, by contrast, a low-number plate might go unnoticed. The difference is rare plates work their magic with familiar faces. Otherwise, their so-called symbolic status disappears. And yet, a newspaper article dated April 6, 1937, from Austin, Texas, discussed the intense debate over the allocation of low-numbered automobile license plates.

Three changes took place in 1942. First, with World War II's arrival, Delaware switched to a single permanent porcelain plate to conserve metal, in line with the rest of the country. Prior to that, most states had issued pairs of tin plates. Second, the DMV that year permanently assigned license number ownership to vehicles, not individuals. Each number remains valid in perpetuity as long as the vehicle's registration is paid. Third, starting that year, the state did not make a general reissue of physical plates for more than four decades. Consequently, some 1980s motorists still had tags made during World War II.

In 1952, the DMV replaced porcelain plates with black stainless-steel plates featuring white embossed letters. The state introduced blue and gold (official state colors) plates in 1957, which remain the default as of this writing.

Delaware's unique system fostered a parallel economy. As older black & white tags grew increasingly rare over time, license-number brokers and auctioneers saw green in black & white.

Classified ads by the 1960s began to transact both vintage plates and low-number registrations. Typically, after procuring a low license number, brokers would have the find reproduced in porcelain-coated steel. This took advantage of the exemption in § 2136(c) of the Delaware code, which allows for the sale of numbers registered prior to 1941, and the manufacture of new plates—as collectors' items —showing those numerals. The black-and-white color scheme of these reproduced plates added cachet for status-seekers.

Big players in the trade of these prized numerals included used-car dealer Jay Hurley of Greenwood and Wilson Auctions in Lincoln. Their services saw increasing demand by the end of the century. "A two-digit would be from $35,000 to $50,000," Hurley told the

News Journal in 1989. "One number? At least $100,000. Unbelievable, right? Nobody, unless they're people who are familiar with tags, believes they bring that kind of money."

Even the Delaware State Lottery got in the game. In March 1993, the grand prize winner of the "Delaware 57" contest won tag number 57, mounted on a fully restored red 1957 Chevrolet Bel Air convertible.

Attraction of low-number license plates in Delaware goes beyond simple alphanumeric markers. First State plates have become cultural icons. They embody family heritage, political influence, and a deep-rooted sense of identity. *Photo: Jordan Irazabal Collection*

Page 63 Twentieth Century Public Figures

Joe Biden, a Delaware senator from 1973 to 2009, played a key role in shaping laws like the Violent Crime Control and Law Enforcement Act and the Violence Against Women Act. His early political career began with his election to the New Castle County Council in 1970. He also oversaw six U.S. Supreme Court confirmation hearings, including the contentious sessions for Robert Bork and Clarence Thomas. Biden's legislative influence extended through his Senate tenure and later in national executive roles.

John Bassett Moore was an American legal scholar, known for exhaustive international law codification. The U.S. government frequently sought his advice on matters pertaining to multinational adjudication. He gained admission to the Delaware Bar in 1883, joined the U.S. Department of State in 1885, and served there until 1891. After more than 30 years on Columbia University's faculty, Moore retired in 1924 as the Hamilton Fish Professor of International Law and Diplomacy. From 1912 to 1938 he was a member of the Permanent Court of Arbitration, The Hague. Among Moore's studies in international law is the monumental *Digest of International Law* (1906). Late in life, he edited the eight-volume compendium of *International Adjudications, Ancient and Modern*.

Senator William V. Roth, Jr. began his distinguished political career at age 49 and served for 30 years. He achieved notable successes in tax reform, government efficiency, and international relations. His 1997 hallmark achievement, the Roth IRA, demonstrates his dedication to promoting retirement savings by offering individuals a tax-advantaged vehicle. The Roth-Kemp tax cuts, a key initiative under President Ronald Reagan, exemplified Roth's commitment to supply-side principles and a limited role for federal oversight in market dynamics.

These cuts stood as a fundamental element of Reagan's fiscal approach and left a lasting imprint on U.S. fiscal policy and the broader 1980s economy. Beyond his work on the Roth IRA and Roth-Kemp tax cuts, Roth was deeply involved in international relations. His leadership in the Finance Committee significantly influenced both national fiscal policy and Delaware's political landscape.

Roth, adept on the world stage, favored strong security alliances and stable global trade relations. He actively demonstrated this through participation in the Trilateral Commission, as well as promotion of the Japan-U.S. Friendship Commission.

The senator's leadership in the influential Finance Committee underscored substantial power. His role as chairman (1995-2001) enabled him to set the agenda, influencing legislative priorities in areas of tax, trade, and social welfare programs.

Roth's Republican stewardship left a legacy on both national and Delaware state politics. The senator's service, spanning over three decades (1971-2001) marks him as one of Delaware's longest-serving politicians.

Elise Ravenel du Pont, primarily a local Delaware politician, extended her influence to the national stage, notably serving as an advisor and fundraiser in a Republican role. During her husband Pierre's tenure as governor from 1977 to 1985, she went beyond the usual First Lady duties.

Du Pont worked in corporate law for several years upon earning her degree from the University of Pennsylvania in 1981. She also took on a vital role at Philadelphia's Franklin Institute, serving on the Board of Managers. Additionally, she was one of the authors updating Delaware's Board of Health nursing home regulations.

As chair of the Governor's Advisory Council on Health during the administrations of Governors Peterson and Tribbitt, du Pont undertook a project to examine the quality of life of the state's migrant farm workers, visiting every such labor camp. After studying the existing regulations, she worked diligently to correct them.

In 1980, du Pont became the first woman of the Delaware World Affairs Council, leading the state's first trade mission to the People's Republic of China. From 1981 to 1984, she served at the Agency for International Development. There, she oversaw a $250 million program to encourage and safeguard developing country investments. This positioned her as a multinational trade facilitator.

Her service also encompassed the public health and education sectors. As Chairman of the State Council on Public Health, she played a principal role in steering policies. Extensive work in these various spheres marked Elise Du Pont as a figure who will be remembered as having transcended traditional First Lady duties.

Jeannette Eckman became the first woman to hold an executive position in Delaware's Republican party when the State Committee appointed her assistant secretary in 1920. She worked for Senator T. Coleman du Pont during his two terms (1921-1922; 1925-1928). Eckman actively participated in the Delaware branch of the Women's Organization for National Prohibition Reform in 1930. This group opposed to dry laws elected her vice chairman by 1933.

Eckman made consequential contributions to women's groups by actively promoting female voting participation. She avidly engaged with local heritage as a member of several Delaware historical and archaeological societies. She was a self-taught historian who mastered her state's history.

The Queen of the Netherlands saluted Eckman in 1938 for leadership in the 300-year anniversary of New Castle's Dutch settlement.

Eckman displayed her dedication to public service by making notable contributions to the Works Progress Administration. She became director in 1941 of the Delaware Federal Writers' Project and the Federal Arts Project under the WPA umbrella.

Eckman authored or edited Delaware guides highlighting local history. She accepted the appointment as director and historian of the New Castle Tercentenary Celebration in 1950. Eckman published *Crane Hook on the Delaware, 1667-1669* in 1957 after twenty years of extensive research. The book covers the period when Crane Hook Church served a parish extending from New Castle to Tinicum, Pennsylvania. The American-Swedish Historical Museum of Philadelphia honored the book with their annual Swedish Award a year later. The University of Delaware reprinted Eckman's 1938 volume *Delaware: A Guide to the First State* in 1955, deeming the book of sufficient historical importance.

Jeannette Eckman wasn't just a pioneering woman in Delaware's Republican party; she was a tireless advocate for women's rights and a key figure in preserving the state's rich history. Through leadership roles in historical and archaeological societies, and her impactful work with the WPA, Eckman's dedication to Delaware's cultural heritage shone brightly.

Wilmingtonian Muriel Gilman dedicated over four decades of service to the United Way of Delaware, becoming the organization's first professional woman. Her sustained diligence led to her appointment as executive vice president in the 1980s. United Way's state chapter grew from 12 to more than 40 staffers coordinating 13,000 volunteers under her leadership. The organization's fundraising campaign increased from $4 million to $15 million. Gilman's passion and her master's in public administration from the University of Delaware drove her to fervently advocate for three causes: housing, children's issues, and midlife nursing education.

Post-retirement, she continued working voluntarily for 20 more years, persistently lobbying the Delaware General Assembly. Gilman consulted for the University of Delaware's College of Health and Nursing Services from 1988 to 2003. She helmed a scholarship fundraising campaign, raising over $1 million, establishing the Muriel E. Gilman Scholarship for Returning Nursing Students.

Additionally, Gilman served on the board of the Delaware Community Foundation, which established the Muriel Gilman Award in tribute to her community service and volunteerism. Governor Michael Castle proclaimed Thursday, December 1, 1988, as Muriel E. Gilman Day in the State of Delaware and urged all Delawareans to recognize her.

The Delaware State Chamber of Commerce in 1995 jointly awarded Gilman and husband Marvin the distinguished Josiah Marvel Cup. The Chamber established the trophy in 1951 to honor a Delawarean making an outstanding contribution to the state, community, and society. Children & Families First, a Wilmington based nonprofit agency providing social, educational, and mental health services, created a Muriel E. Gilman Family Advocacy Award. She had first served there as advocacy chairperson, then vice president in 2007, and for years on the board of directors. The Hall of Fame of Delaware Women inducted Muriel Gilman in 2005.

Muriel E. Gilman's four-decade service with the United Way of Delaware and her advocacy in housing, children's issues, and nursing education reflect a deep commitment to social causes. Moreover, savvy stewardship in fundraising and volunteerism left a lasting impact on Delaware's community services.

Twentieth-century history has been memorably shaped by these six trailblazers, whose resilience, innovation, and leadership have profoundly impacted Delaware and beyond. Their diverse legacies, rooted in decades of wisdom and depth of insight, demonstrate how individuals from a small state can influence national and global affairs. Simply put, each and every one articulated with their lips, their pens, their words as they reached out to varied communities and told their stories both at home and abroad. *Gilman watercolor by Theresa (Terre) Walton, for the Delaware Women's Hall of Fame; Du Pont painting by David Larned, Office of the Governor/State of Delaware; Biden photo by AP Images; Moore photo from "The World's Work (1921)" by Paul Thompson; Eckman photo public domain/Wikipedia; Roth photo public domain/Wikipedia*

Page 64 Nanticoke Powwows

Starting in 1922, Chief Wyniaco, in collaboration with anthropologist Dr. Frank C. Speck, initiated Thanksgiving Day powwows. These events, drawing both tourists and Native American guests, became platforms for cultural exchanges and historical ceremonies.

In his 1927 powwow address, Chief Wyniaco spoke about Powhatan's leadership, "whose rule extended over 40 tribes from the James River to the Potomac River." The chief lauded him for his cooperation with the early European settlers. He also praised Powhatan's major decision to marry his daughter, Pocahontas, to John Rolfe, symbolizing a cemented alliance between the two peoples.

Chief Wyniaco reflected on the crucial roles of leaders like Powhatan and Massasoit, the chief of the Wampanoags, in altering the course of American history. He concluded by noting Powhatan's long-lasting friendship with the English, inadvertently allowing their power to grow.

Powwow revivals were not, as one might think, merely social gatherings. They symbolized a renaissance of indigenous culture. The Association extended invitations to respected tribal leaders like Chief Strong Wolf of the Ojibway Tribe and Princess Tantaquidgeon of the Mohican Tribe. The gesture demonstrated a desire to foster an enriching cultural dialogue. Dr. Speck's affiliation with the University of Pennsylvania opened doors for other academics from there and the University of Delaware, allowing them to participate and make contributions to anthropology.

Following the formative dynamic years, the Association entered a more insular phase beginning with the 1928 stewardship of Chief Charles Cullen Clark (Little Owl). Chief Little Owl's leadership approach embodied a quiet resolve, a strategy necessary for the times. He reminisced about his Nanticoke ancestors at a 1934 Thanksgiving Day powwow. There was a time, he said, when they roamed the woods and waters of Delaware, vividly recalling the abundance of wild fowl and seafood. These natural resources once pervaded Rehoboth and Indian River Bays, as well as the marshes surrounding them. He told of how his people had been able to live in peace and contentment; to hunt and fish and live in abundance. Speaking of the plentitude of wild fowl foods in those early days, Chief Little Owl said that this was because the marshes and waters were kept brackish from the inlet, which had not become clogged. "Even in fairly recent years," said Chief Little Owl, "the members of my tribe who still live along the shores of Indian River in Eastern Sussex County made comfortable livings from the waters and marshes, by crabbing, fishing, oystering and trapping."

The tribe focused over the next four decades on community cohesion and local land ownership, mirroring their external retreat.

Chief Little Owl's 1971 death signified a turning point. His son Kenneth Clark (Red Deer) ushered in what can best be described as a rebirth. Red Deer's advocacy, particularly for non-reservation tribes, symbolized a shift in the Association's stance. "I know less than my father did; and my kids will know a great deal less than I about our past. Once you lose the knowledge of the heritage or the language, you have nothing," he told the *News Journal*.

This sentiment underscored to the tribe the urgent need for a proactive approach to preserving and sharing the Nanticoke legacy. "It was a pivotal moment," he said, "but the people realized it was important to preserve our heritage. It was like a renaissance. The young people wanted to know about the tribe, the traditional dances and Indian dress."

Notably, the late 1970s saw the Nanticoke Indian Association (NIA) sponsor an inaugural parade as well as secure a federal grant. This $29,000 funding facilitated higher education for five tribal members and financed a census of the local Indian population.

The 1978 relaunch of the Nanticoke Indian Powwow reinvigorated the NIA. Their celebration was an educational endeavor, striving to dismantle Hollywood's clichéd representations of Native Americans.

They wanted to present a more authentic and complex view of their culture and traditions. They channeled financial gains from the event into the creation of a Nanticoke Indian Museum in Millsboro. The NIA established the facility in 1984 — the only Native American museum in the state and one of only 13 Nanticoke sites recognized nationwide as a historical landmark.

Ever since its revival, the Nanticoke Indian Powwow has been an annual beacon of cultural pride, seamlessly weaving the past into the present and ensuring the continuity of this vibrant tradition.

The NIA stands today as both a guardian of the past and a participant in the current era. Their history features visionary chiefs, scholarly collaborations, access to federal grants, and public events. The Association demonstrates how adaptability can sustain a culture through varying seasons. NIA's past offers a case study in the preservation of indigenous heritage: navigating cultural identity, community involvement, and societal engagement. *pow-wow circle photo: Delaware Public Archives; Chief Russell Clark and wife Florence: National Museum of the American Indian Archive Center, Smithsonian Institution*

Page 65 Delaware State Housing Authority

Locales across the country felt the impact of these policies in the form of mass foreclosures and social disarray. World War II intervened, halting civilian construction and leading to a pent-up demand for homes. The FHA and Veterans Administration (VA) ac tively steered the reconfiguration of American suburbs in the post-war era through their insured mortgages and financing programs, which were specifically designed to address the housing backlog.

Developers incorporated the FHA-endorsed subdivision regulations and restrictive covenants directly into legal contracts. The move effectively institutionalized discrimination by prohibiting the sale of houses to certain minority groups, with African Americans facing the most notable exclusions. Alongside this, the VA loan program, designed to assist returning veterans in purchasing homes by spreading mortgage payments over a 30-year period, also became enmeshed in these frameworks. Despite an intent to help veterans, the VA's insured mortgage program inadvertently perpetuated bigotry by adhering to similar restrictions.

The 1950s witnessed a further shift in the federal landscape. The FHA launched its "Campaign for Economy Housing" (CEH) with the aim of balancing racial disparities. This initiative, though well-intentioned, led to mixed outcomes.

Developments like Wilmington's Dunleith Estates, targeting African American veterans and structured by private developers to use VA financing, marked a positive step. But the same era also saw the displacement and demolition of predominantly Black enclaves. This contributed to Wilmington's loss of nearly 14,000 residents, leading to city center neglect.

The downtown area of Wilmington once hosted a diverse mix of social classes and races living in close quarters. However, the proliferation of federally backed mortgages catalyzed suburban "white flight," relegating African Americans to working-class zones. These developments, along with the redlining practices, left a deep scar on the metropolitan fabric, segregating and isolating communities.

The Civil Rights Movement of the early 1960s intensified in response to inner city decline, rising poverty, and growing awareness of Black neighborhood isolation. This situation necessitated a more local urban planning strategy.

The assassination of Dr. Martin Luther King, Jr. in 1968 and the subsequent national unrest, particularly on Wilmington's East Side, marked a turning point. Delaware authorities in October, responding to escalating social challenges, established the Delaware State Housing Authority (DSHA).

The new agency sought to address the critical needs of affordable dwellings for low and moderate-income families. As a housing finance agency, DSHA provides loans and grants to both for-profit and non-profit housing sponsors, and applies for federal subsidies.

Today, the DSHA grapples with the legacies of past policies, including the complexities of VA lending programs and their historical role in perpetuating segregation, particularly in Wilmington. The authority's continuing work, which includes providing loans to mortgage lenders so they can, in turn, make new residential mortgage loans, and issuing bonds and notes, underscores the urgency of addressing these disparities. Such efforts highlight the evolving nature of city development and the enduring impact of historical housing policies. *Wilmington, Delaware Real Property Inventory Map: Research Division of the Federal Housing Administration*

Page 66 Punkin Chunkin

Three years in, the organizers anticipated only a half-dozen catapults—a medieval invention used to hurl objects. In this quirky modern version, these dischargers were designed to propel pumpkins as far as possible. Entries needed to be officially measured and were expected to remain intact until they hit the ground. The early acts of "chunkin" relied on the power of one human operator.

Melson and Thompson still did not require any formal registration despite a growing list of rules. Event spokesman Harry Lackhove speculated that a throw of 1,000 feet might clinch the 1989 gathering's first place. The prize was no more than "a cap or T-shirt and the right to crow for a year," he shared with the *News Journal*.

Participation and interest surged by 1991. Approximately 5,000 spectators had gathered to watch 12 entrants. Competitors flung 8-10 lb. pumpkins using a mix of wooden catapults, trebuchets (medieval siege weapons), and a bit later, pneumatic air cannons.

The Delaware event soon captivated a widespread audience. The following year, the allure and mechanical challenge of hurling a pumpkin drew between 7,500 to 10,000 spectators. Many traveled from as far as Canada and Alaska to witness the spectacle, filled with wonderment at the sight of gourds soaring through the sky.

State tourist officials noticed the contest's rapid growth. Governor Tom Carper presented the 1993 Governor's Tourism Award to the hurlers, honoring Punkin Chunkin as Delaware's outstanding special event. Organizers subdivided the categories, introducing human-powered-only and youth divisions. A pumpkin recipe contest added another layer of charm.

Female competitors participated in the Punkin Chunkin championship right from the beginning, but for a decade, no woman had clinched the coveted top prize for distance. Only the male competitors wore the distinctive jack-o'-lantern gold-and-diamond championship ring (introduced in 1996). Yet, the spirit of competition between the sexes remained undeterred.

Brenda Sennett, operating an air cannon for team "Poor and Hungry," set a women's record with a shot spanning 3,308 feet, marking the longest distance to date. Brenda, along with her husband Wayne, participated each year in a circuit of five different pumpkin "shoots." The team "Hormone Blaster" went on to set the record for the farthest pumpkin chunk attained by women in the competition history in 2013. They achieved a distance of 4,382.96 feet in the Adult Female Air category.

Founders Trey Melson and Bill Thompson themselves stood as formidable competitors. These two hometown heroes seized the top spot five times each in the contest's first decade.

Delaware's dominance faced a challenge when competition from Morton, Illinois entered the growing fray. Morton's claim to fame, Libby's pumpkin processing plant, produces a consequential share of the nation's canned pumpkin. The Land of Lincoln team, demonstrating profound pumpkin prowess, unveiled an 18-ton, 100-foot-long air-powered cannon mounted on an old cement mixer. They stole the 1996 title from Delaware's finest using this contraption, managing to win again in 1998.

In 2002, for the first time, the Discovery Channel televised Punkin Chunkin, introducing this unique Delawarean tradition to millions of nationwide viewers. Starting in 2008 and continuing until 2016, the Science Channel aired the contest.

Sadly, the event faced a major setback that year. Suzanne Dakessian, a producer at the Science Channel, suffered air cannon injuries, and the station immediately canceled the Punkin Chunkin special. The following August, Dakessian filed a civil lawsuit against the organization, its leaders, the state Department of Natural Resources and Environmental Control and the farm where the event was held. Her two-year litigation, combined with other factors, halted the beloved event. A federal judge subsequently dismissed the claim in January 2019, but Punkin Chunkin in Delaware was effectively over.

The Punkin Chunkin contest's rise and resilience reflects the strength of community traditions. The Delaware get-together party spirit remains unbroken, waiting for the next big blow out.

Page 67 Credit Card Industry

The ripple was substantial, with 13,000 direct jobs created and an additional 7,000 jobs generated in non-banking sectors such as food service, retail, and hospitality. By 1991, the state had become home to thirty-one credit card and wholesale banks.

Bank franchise taxes were added to the state's coffers, skyrocketing to $70 million from a meager $2 million a decade earlier. The FCDA had flung the doors wide open for credit card issuers. Blowing off the hinges further, the state passed the Consumer Credit Bank Act in 1983, this time catering specifically to smaller regional banks.

The First State reaped palpable economic dividends. Economists at the University of Delaware conducted a study that revealed a 15 percent annual growth rate from 1983 through the first quarter of 1989. The financial deregulations drove this astonishing rise.

"Delaware offers the same financial sophistication as New York and has some financial incentives to boot," said Nina Keesling, of the Dover-based Delaware Development Office, in 1990.

"As we solicit international holding companies, we are getting them used to Delaware ... in hopes that they too may bring other operations to the state," said the financial institutions specialist. "Those who have the first foothold get the lion's share of the market."

Fast-forward to the turn of the millennium. Delaware's FinTech sector metamorphosed into an indispensable pillar of the state's economy. One of the most iconic financial institutions, Wilmington Trust, exemplified this vitality. Founded in 1903 as the original FinTech innovator, Wilmington Trust remained a major player for 108 years before being acquired by M&T Bank.

The industry, now offering nearly 34,000 jobs and swollen to include more than three dozen banks, became the state's largest employer. "To see what it has grown into today is just unbelievable," expressed David Bakerian from the Delaware Bankers Association.

The financial sector's trajectory was not always upward. A series of 1998 mergers saw a shrinkage in the ranks of Delaware banks. Yet the industry's dominance held firm, contributing that year to 13.5 percent of the state's economy. The fiscal year 1999 alone saw the banks paying more than $259 million in bank franchise taxes, solidifying their position as a financial linchpin in the state's economy.

The FCDA legislation had far-reaching effects, impacting the banking sectors beyond state borders. "[The industry is] very significant to the state in terms of employment and bank franchise tax revenue," Robert Glen, Delaware state bank commissioner, told the *News Journal* in early 2000. "And the banks are very big contributors to the community in being good corporate citizens."

As the twentieth century ended, Delaware bankers further consolidated their position on the American financial map. In 1999, the state passed legislation allowing foreign banks to designate Delaware as U.S. headquarters for expansion nationwide. The state's favorable trust laws also began drawing in limited-purpose trust companies and major insurers, expanding Delaware's assets portfolio.

Two of the nation's largest, most aggressive card marketers were based in Wilmington by 2000: First USA Bank, a unit of Chicago-based Bank One, and MBNA, the nation's third-largest card supplier. Eight of the nation's top ten credit card issuers were in Delaware or had large operations there. More than 60 percent of the world's credit cards were issued from the state. The First State has remained a major player in the credit card industry, continuing to host an overwhelming portion of the U.S. bank card market.

Delaware's banking rise from 1981 to 2000 illustrates the impact of strategic legislative initiatives coupled with a conducive business environment. The sector propelled the state to reshape its economic destiny. *Photo of Governor du Pont: Delaware Public Archives*

Page 68 Estuary Protection

The decisions we make today will determine whether our sanctuary continues to thrive or dwindles into a distant memory.

Wetland habitats excel as natural filtration systems, safeguarding larger bodies of water. The once-abundant oysters have played an important role in Delaware Bay's renewing process. A single oyster can filter as much as 50 gallons per day, removing pollutants and also oxygenating marine life. Furthermore, the Bay's extensive swamps act as protective storm buffers for inland communities. Fewer toxins translate into healthier fisheries that sustain both commercial and recreational activities. Bay angling grounds contribute hundreds of millions of dollars each year to the state's economy.

Delaware Bay, celebrated for remarkable biodiversity, stands amid the world's most vibrant natural marshlands. The highly productive ecosystem serves as a sanctuary for over 130 fish species. The wetlands play a key role as a breeding habitat for horseshoe crabs.

The thriving horseshoe crab population, in turn, sustains a complex food web that supports thousands of shorebirds, including red knots, sandpipers, and black-bellied plovers. These birds, embarking from the southern extremities of South America, arrive in Delaware Bay by late May, finding a critical stopover for rest and nourishment.

Among these migratory species, the red knot distinguishes itself by engaging in one of the avian world's most extensive journeys. Originating from Tierra del Fuego at the southern tip of South America, red knots traverse to their breeding grounds in the High Arctic, covering distances that can reach between 9,000 and 9,500 miles. This remarkable feat underscores not only the endurance of the red knot but also highlights the ecological significance of Delaware Bay. The bay offers essential respite and sustenance, vital for the birds as they prepare for the subsequent leg of their migration to the Arctic.

Upon replenishing their energy reserves in Delaware Bay, these shorebirds continue northward to their Arctic breeding grounds. From these northern reaches, they embark on a return journey south in the fall, completing an annual cycle both breathtaking and essential for survival.

The Delaware Estuary has faced human-inflicted harm over the years due to excessive fishing, dredging, and environmental contamination from runoffs. In the late 1890s, the Delaware River had the largest annual commercial shad harvest of any river on the Atlantic Coast, with estimates of up to 19 million pounds a year. These numbers plummeted by the early twentieth century due to unsustainable fishing practices and the deterioration of water quality.

Infrastructure projects, such as dam construction, have further depleted these vital ecosystems. For example, New York City built an upstate reservoir in the 1960s and the faraway move altered the Delaware River's headwaters. This disruption in freshwater flows had a cascade of ecological effects, most notably impacting Delaware Bay species such as the Eastern Oyster.

In 1988, the Environmental Protection Agency (EPA) designated the Delaware Estuary, which includes Delaware Bay, as one of 28 National Estuary Program sites. The implementation, under 1987 amendments to the Clean Water Act, was intended to counteract the most devastating damage to flora and fauna.

The program led to cooperative efforts among various stakeholders. Federal agencies like the EPA collaborated with state governments. Non-profit organizations such as the Partnership for the Delaware Estuary also joined in the fray. Together, they sought to restore native habitats and improve water quality.

Conservation endeavors included a practice called *oyster gardening* to regrow their declining populations. Special hatcheries raised oyster "seeds" and "spat" until large enough to survive when introduced into the Delaware Bay. Further efforts encompassed multistate campaigns to clean up PCBs and other industrial pollutants.

Yet challenges remain.

In light of the continued need to protect Delaware Bay's tidal wetlands, the pioneering work of conservationists like Ted Harvey has become increasingly instructive. His initiatives through Delaware Wild Lands, Inc., underscored the importance of individual commitment to environmental stewardship.

A majority of Delaware's business community continues to believe that environmental regulations threaten both profits and job growth. Some environmentalists might counter that what is good for business is no doubt bad for the environment.

Both positions are not necessarily so. The economy of Rehoboth Beach, for example, owes a lot to the environmental regulations that keep ocean waters and beaches clean. How many tourists would visit the resort community if the Atlantic were polluted?

Cost and risk assessments evaluating the financial burden placed on the private sector by environmental regulations must be weighed against the public harm caused by the lack of those rules. This back-and-forth balancing act will be a given in the future as the state examines the need for additional conservation policies and their resulting impact on Delaware's economy.

America, more broadly, bears a collective obligation to preserve the tidal wetlands of Delaware Bay, given the importance of both an unparalleled ecological and economic value. The estuary's vital habitats rest on a fragile symmetry that we have disrupted but also possess the power to restore. Custody, entrusted by generations past, is a legacy citizens, conservationists, and legislators are compelled to uphold and pass on to those who follow. *Marsh photo: Peter Schilling Photography/Flickr; Lighthouse sunset: Tony Pratt/ Flickr*

Page 69 Hispanic Immigration

Asked by the *News Journal* what he did for fun, Alcantara replied: "Nothing."

Varying degrees of population concentration exist among different Sussex County subgroups. Nationalities congregate based on place of origin. For example, Guatemalans coalesce around Georgetown. By 2000, Hispanics made up 32% of that town's residents.

Hispanic immigrants include, contrary to common stereotypes, both rural and urban populations, with diverse educational backgrounds. Urban immigrants often assimilate more quickly and regain their social standing, while working-class immigrants usually stay within ethnic enclaves.

The immigrants maintain strong connections with their home countries, often sending remittances that contribute to those economies. Employment opportunities in low-skilled jobs are the main attraction to Sussex County. Companies have adapted by offering language training and promoting skilled workers.

The evolving demographic landscape reshaped the county and simultaneously highlighted critical issues surrounding legal status and immigration policies. Misconceptions about legitimacy abound, but most immigrants in Sussex County have legal documentation. U.S. immigration laws and policies have had a complex impact on their population. The flow north channels the confluence of laws, societal needs, and opportunities. These collective factors affect both foreign nationals and their United States descendants.

America has grappled with a steady stream of hurdles in both immigration and refugee policy. The 1980 Refugee Act established a more organized framework, allowing for the annual entry of 50,000 exiled persons. The Act also offered a pathway for 5,000 individuals to apply for asylum. Cold War politics led to inconsistencies in U.S. treatment of Central American refugees. America often favored individuals fleeing socialist regimes. Meanwhile, those escaping right-wing dictatorships frequently faced rejection.

In the 1980s, El Salvador and Guatemala faced violence and civil wars, which resulted in mass displacement. Many fled poverty, repression, and discrimination. U.S. foreign policy further exacerbated these situations, at times enabling the crises to fester. Activists and legal advocates reacted by suing the Immigration and Naturalization Service. A resulting 1990 settlement granted temporary protective status to refugees without offering amnesty.

Although a Guatemalan peace accord was signed in December 1996 to still the 36-year civil war, refugees continued to fear for their lives should they go back home. Alejandro Tzan Vicente, a 46-year-old former police officer from Totonicapan, declared in a 1998 interview with the *News Journal*, "Returning is no longer an option for us."

Subsequent legislation created a divided path to permanent residency. Some laws favored Nicaraguans and Cubans over Salvadorans and Guatemalans. Changes in the late 1990s began to equalize the conditions for these diverse groups. Sussex County, thanks to late twentieth century immigration, confronts challenges such as housing shortages, language barriers, and legal status. The largest employers—poultry plants—do not offer shelter, complicating the already limited dwelling options. Language barriers render immigrants susceptible to exploitation. Increased police patrols, added bilingual officers, and similar initiatives are called for. Two predominant viewpoints exist regarding undocumented immigrants. One advocates for stricter border controls and criminalization of undocumented workers. The other promotes normalization of immigrant status.

Sussex County reflects America's evolving identity of changing demographics and immigration policies. This story underscores the nation's efforts to integrate humanitarian ideals with workforce development and social cohesion. Southern Delaware's history pro vides lessons for embracing diversity as a fundamental element of our national fabric. *Poultry workers photo Nati Harnik/AP Photo*

Page 70 Tourism Industry

DSTS aimed to build on water-themed tourism and develop Delaware into a well-rounded hub for culture and recreation. The state conducted the first-ever cost-benefit analysis in 1977 to evaluate sector profitability. This groundbreaking study generated such curiosity from other states, intrigued by the data, that they began buying copies. The same year, Pierre S. du Pont became governor.

Du Pont, encouraged by positive outcomes, threw full support behind expanding the initiative. He actively invested in tourism promotion and elevated the industry's role in Delaware's economic strategy. The 1978 budget stood at a mere $78,000, the lowest across the nation. The governor bolstered the allocation to a much healthier $460,000.

DSTS shifted focus under Mathewson's leadership. New Castle County lacked child-friendly attractions. Therefore, DSTS administrators redirected their marketing strategy to target young childless couples and "empty nesters." These groups would appreciate the county's cultural museums, historical landmarks, and scenic landscapes, without the need for child-oriented entertainment.

Building on this core demographic, the "Small Wonder" advertising campaign zoomed in further. The drive focused initially on individuals with a median middle-class salary who lived within 300 miles of the state. Mathewson later narrowed the campaign's focus. Despite drawing tourists from faraway locations, the primary goal remained to pull visitors from nearby metropolitan areas.

Delaware lacked a major airport, posing a challenge in attracting tourists who would first need to fly into Baltimore or Philadelphia. Wilmington Airport could only handle small corporate jets at the time.

A study taken in 1979 indicated that 360 million tourist dollars flowed into the state that year. The analysis also determined that 15,000 direct jobs and 19,000 indirect ones resulted thanks to tourism.

The legislature in October 1981 created the Delaware Development Office (DDO) to assume a dual mission to promote both state tourism and industrial development. Director Nathan Hayward ousted Mathewson in favor of "an expert in the travel field."

The state increased DDO's budget the following year to $471,000 and diversified advertising avenues. The office did not have the money to advertise on TV but did use the glossy pages of several well-known magazines to spread the word. Ads appeared in *Southern Living* magazine as part of DDO's campaign to make people more aware of Delaware. In one print piece, the camera captured a long-necked heron poised for flight at the Bombay Hook National Wildlife Refuge, seizing the precise moment before the bird soared into the air. Above this, a caption read "Wing It." A line beneath the picture urged those who lived outside the First State to "catch the next flight." The Bombay Hook ad also circulated in such magazines as *Americana* and *Travel Holiday*.

DDO spent an additional $12 million across various agencies to accommodate incoming tourists. For instance, the state earmarked $32,000 for certain medical examiner expenses such as covering the costs of autopsies and locating relatives when individuals died while passing through Delaware.

Southern Delaware, particularly the beach resorts, already boasted a high return on advertising rate—around 75%—and therefore required less marketing intervention. So, Jan Geddes, the new DDO acting travel director, set her primary advertising sights on northern Delaware. She specifically highlighted the region known as "Chateau Country" in 1982 promotional efforts. This area boasts not only the renowned du Pont estates of Hagley Museum and Winterthur but also other must-see attractions like Longwood Gardens, Granogue, Mount Cuba Center, and Nemours Mansion and Gardens, all open to the public.

Geddes cultivated relationships with travel writers to increase Delaware's visibility. This strategy yielded both immediate and enduring results: A *Glamour* magazine feature in 1982 led to over a thousand information calls. By 1994, northern Delaware claimed 12 of the state's 20 most visited sites, from Longwood Gardens to Wilmington's 1871 Grand Opera House.

Expanding the scope of their efforts, DDO aimed to maximize tight resources by focusing on specific overseas demographics. Delaware extended an open invitation to the United Kingdom and Germany, countries whose airlines had direct flights to Philadelphia. The largest number of tourists came from Canada, with Switzerland and Japan rounding out the top five visiting nations.

Under Jan Geddes' expanding leadership, Delaware tourism experienced an uplift. "My educational background in business marketing with a minor in graphic arts and design helped immensely when I was the Director of Tourism," she recalled.

Outsiders once taunted "Dela-WHERE???" Eventually the slur evolved into a badge of honor for First Staters. Residents embraced the slogan on t-shirts and bumper stickers. Rather than an insult, the phrase came to represent pride in Delaware's unique locale. The state shed any lingering obscurity through dedicated investments and was now appreciated as a vibrant and sought-after destination. Delaware's cultural, historical, and recreational attractions drew wider audiences. This complete re-imagining symbolized a state so

Page 71 Wilmington Religious Leaders

Finding his ministry in neighborhood building, Balducelli established the Padua Academy, founded a senior citizens' home called The Antonian, and created a Pennsylvania countryside summer retreat for children named St. Anthony's in the Hills. He had long dreamed of a camp where kids could enjoy nature. "When I came to this country," he reminisced, "the kids were playing in the rectory and had nowhere to go. I said, 'What we need is a camp.'"

Balducelli's revitalization of St. Anthony's Italian Festival brought a slice of Italian "gioia di vita" to Wilmington, creating a vibrant space for social gatherings and cultural celebrations.

During a 2013 birthday interview, Balducelli stated the festivities unite Delawareans across faiths and nationalities. "The festival answers a basic human need to gather and talk," he told reporters. "People need to meet at more than just weddings and funerals." He explained the pageant also extends a welcome homecoming for those who have moved away. "Every once in a while, someone comes along who literally transforms a community," remarked Vice President Joe Biden in a heartfelt eulogy, "—and that's exactly what Father Roberto Balducelli did."

Brother Ronald Giannone carried on his Capuchin Franciscan order's eight-century tradition of serving the world's poorest, inspired by St. Francis of Assisi. In 1977, he founded Delmarva's first emergency shelter for homeless and destitute women. The Mary Mother of Hope House, expanded to become the Ministry of Caring, has since served more than 7,000 women. The friar introduced dining rooms, housing facilities, and employment services with inspired conviction and a guiding vision. Giannone also launched medical outreach and affordable infant care programs. He believed that "the poor should never be treated poorly."

"I don't believe anyone wants to stand in a bread line," Giannone said. In 1999, Delaware's State Chamber of Commerce awarded him the Marvel Cup, an award for outstanding service to the people of Delaware presented beginning in 1951. The honor recognized Giannone both as a minister to the marginalized as well as a social entrepreneur. Prior recipients included such notables as Russell W. Peterson, a former governor; J. Caleb Boggs, a U.S. senator and governor; Pierre S. du Pont IV, a former governor; and Irving Shapiro, a former CEO of DuPont. Brother Ronald Giannone's efforts had set a high standard for how faith-based organizations contribute to social justice.

Sister Jeanne Cashman dedicated 18 years to teaching as an Ursuline nun. She turned to social welfare in 1987, founding Sojourner's Place. The goal was to help train individuals with skills that could enable them to climb out of poverty. Cashman noted at its start that "We have a lot of hopes for this program, and you always have fears when you start something new." She pointed out "There is not a shelter like this in the state. One of the things we learned from the old shelter is that homeless people have a variety of needs, a lot of which are widely scattered in the community and not always accessible to the homeless. So, we thought by putting everything in the building that they would have right here what they needed to get rehabbed."

The center created a unique, unprecedented shelter. Cashman's statewide efforts and activism, touching upon women's rights, racial equality, and affordable housing issues, earned high honors. Her work opened new avenues through social service outreach for addressing systemic hurdles. The pioneering nun built up the well-being of countless community members along the way. Delaware Women's Hall of Fame inducted her in 2003.

Chattanooga native Maurice Moyer earned his Masters of Divinity from Lincoln University Theological Seminary. He took up his pastoral role at Wilmington's Community Presbyterian Church in 1955. Reverend Moyer served for 46 years and became the first Black moderator of the New Castle Presbytery from 1963-64.

The minister played a strong role in Delaware's civil rights movement. In 1963, he led the charge to change the Innkeeper's Act of Delaware. This legislation gave hotel and restaurant owners the authority to turn away any unwanted customers. Though appearing neutral, the law commonly resulted in racial discrimination in day-to-day enforcement. Moyer's successful advocacy had a lasting impact on advancing racial equality. His push led to the repeal of the Innkeepers Law and the outlawing of discrimination based on race, color, religion, or national origin in "places of public accommodation." Governor Jack Markell honored Moyer upon his death in 2012. Flags flew at half-staff in Wilmington and New Castle County.

Giannone, Balducelli, Cashman, and Moyer unified diverse groups across Wilmington with a shared mission of enhancing the human condition. Giannone's Ministry of Caring and Balducelli's church initiatives offered immediate relief, while Cashman and Moyer pursued systemic change for long-term impact.

Their collective efforts transcended denominational lines and galvanized local governments, congregations, and nonprofits. This mobilization fostered an ethos of responsibility and compassion towards the marginalized. Each story makes all our hearts beat a little faster. *Photo Emmanuel Dining Room: courtesy First Unitarian Church of Wilmington Delaware; photos of Maurice Moyer and Community Presbyterian Church interior courtesy Presbyterian Historical Society*

Page 72 Digital Medical Technology

The 1973 release of computed tomography in the United States marked the first of several pioneering innovations. Nicknamed the "CAT" scanner, this three-dimensional X-ray provided in-depth anatomical details. Wilmington Medical Center installed Delaware's inaugural CT scanner in 1976 for over half a million dollars. The device found widespread adoption in both hospital departments and outpatient practices.

Another breakthrough came in the mid-1980s with magnetic resonance imaging (MRI). Unlike CT scanners, MRI uses radio waves and magnets to create detailed images of organs and tissues, offering a safer alternative that avoids radiation. However, the high cost limited their initial accessibility. Christiana Hospital led the way in Delaware by acquiring the first MRI scanner in 1987.

Radiologist Dr. John S. Wills told of a patient sent there that year by an orthopedic surgeon for a scan of a thigh injury, first diagnosed as a pulled muscle, that was not improving. The MRI assessment showed that the man had ripped a tendon directly off the bone, an injury that had to be repaired surgically. "No other imaging could have told that," Wills said. Christiana Hospital's early adoption set a trend, with other facilities across the state soon adding MRI capabilities to their services.

Seeing the rising demand, Papastavros' Associates Medical Imaging entered the burgeoning digital MDIC industry in 1993 as an early player. They opened facilities focused exclusively on the new imaging services. At the time, this Newark-based private group practice comprised five radiologists and had been offering X-ray services for 35 years. Their specialization in these new offerings allowed them to capture enormous cost efficiencies. "This is the greatest thing that ever came to our practice since Roentgen discovered the X-ray," Dr. Christos Papastavros said, arguing the CT scan diagnosed conditions that previous tests failed. "When you need it, you need it badly." The profitable venture proved that freestanding centers are a viable business model. This paved the way for the rapid expansion of advanced medical imaging systems via dedicated community providers.

A 1994 study found that Delaware's adoption rate drastically outpaced many states—18 MRI machines per million residents, compared to a median ratio of 8.9 across 20 states and Washington, D.C. This rapid diffusion highlighted both the financial success of imaging services in Delaware, as well as rising consumer demand.

Alongside MRI and CT, the state also saw the integration of PET (Positron Emission Tomography) scanners into various healthcare facilities. PET scanners use a special dye containing radioactive tracers to visualize and measure metabolic processes. This is crucial in detecting conditions like cancer by providing detailed cellular-level insights.

The swift adoption and proliferation of MRI units, CT, and PET scanners in the First State stemmed from favorable demographics and economic conditions. The state's low-tax climate attracts financially secure retirees, whose needs increase demand for advanced healthcare like high-resolution imaging. Moreover, health-savvy pensioners often have comprehensive insurance policies that incentivize providers to bill for expensive diagnostic procedures.

Major Delaware corporations like DuPont, MBNA, and AstraZeneca likewise drive imaging growth. Known for strong employee benefits, these companies contribute to a robust local healthcare market receptive to advanced services. Their presence plays a crucial role in the rapid regional expansion of medical imaging.

Renowned medical research facilities such as the Delaware Medical Research Institute at Christiana Hospital and the Delaware Institute of Medical Education and Research in Dover foster the adoption of advanced medical devices. These organizations both fuel academic breakthroughs and train medical professionals. Such specialized learning ensures that healthcare providers can effectively use the latest medical technology.

Delaware's modest size facilitates the state-wide acceptance of new medical applications. Each locale can smoothly navigate policy changes, unencumbered by large district complexities. This efficiency fuels both funding and regulatory approval. The state's integration of digital innovations revolutionized patient diagnosis while also elevating the healthcare economy. Deploying these visionary technologies created a domino effect. The effort boosted employment in medical technology and spurred local research and development. This solidified Delaware's hub for innovative healthcare services. *Aerial photo of Delaware Division hospital of Wilmington Medical Center courtesy Hagley Museum and Library; Diasonics, Inc. MRI scanner: UC San Francisco, Library, Special Collections*

Page 73 Biotechnology Institute

Weir rose to become a vice president for global research during a subsequent five-year stint with DuPont. He planned to leverage regional scientific triumphs, gaining financial commitment from DuPont for DBI. Hercules Inc., a Wilmington-based chemical and munitions manufacturing company, pledged $1 million, marking early private sector investment in the joint venture.

The director's ambitions did not stop at merely hosting research endeavors. He envisaged an incubator-style program to help fledgling companies share research facilities and alleviate hefty R&D costs. Stakeholders hoped to attract venture capital and seed funding to nourish the institute's nascent projects. This echoed a national trend, with analogous hubs in Boston and San Diego.

The first faculty recruit from the University of Delaware, in 1999, was biologist Dr. Janine Sherrier. She brought expertise in plant-molecular biology and specialized in bridging academic insight with industrial application. Sherrier, then an assistant professor at UD's Department of Plant and Soil Sciences, had an extensive background in *proteomics* — the study of protein function, plant development, and plant molecular biology. Her research efforts focused on nitrogen.

Many crops are supplemented with nitrogen-rich fertilizers for optimal growth because of soil nitrogen depletion. She said her research could "potentially reduce the amount of fertilizer that is necessary for use on soil, which would be beneficial for the environment. It may also lead to improvement of more commercially important plants, such as soybeans or peanuts."

DBI planned to bring 20 additional faculty members on board over a three-year period, but hiring challenges loomed. Lack of qualified manpower posed a continual threat, pointed out Scott Reynolds from the Delaware Information Technology Association. He underscored the risk of high-tech companies relocating to the state if the local talent pool remained shallow. The fervent quest for experienced workers mirrored a nationwide scramble.

The broader conversation centered around both the potential and pitfalls of biotechnology. William F. Kirk, head of DuPont's agriculture and bioscience division, boldly predicted that genetically modified organisms (GMOs) would have the power to reshape Delaware, and the world. Genetically engineered seeds would produce larger, nutritionally enhanced crops, on less land. That breakthrough could be used to feed the estimated 800 million people worldwide who are chronically malnourished. "The opportunities in biotechnology are exciting and large, but not without controversy," Kirk acknowledged.

Critics argued that the long-term impacts of GMOs on health and the environment were not yet fully understood. There were concerns about the potential for allergic reactions, gene transfer to non-target species, and the unintended consequences of tampering with the natural genetic makeup of plants. The ownership of GMO seed patents by large corporations such as Monsanto raised additional issues about the control of the global food supply. These pitfalls included farmer dependency on patented seeds and the ethics of making essential agricultural technology exclusive. Furthermore, skepticism towards human-based genetic engineering casts a long shadow. The societal dismay on the unknowns of human cloning and "designer babies" grew louder. "The genie is out of the bottle, and it has to be managed," Weir said.

DBI's six-story edifice stood tall in Newark by the end of 2000. A new era of scientific inquiry and economic aspiration dawned. The venture positioned Delaware at the crossroads of global biotechnological innovation and ethical discourse. Director Weir displayed clear optimism regarding Delaware's emerging stature in the life sciences. "This field has a tremendous history," he added. He emphasized the region's impact by stating, "If you took away this area's discoveries from the marketplace, this would be a different world. Some people will say that this could be the industrial revolution of the 21st century." Weir also harbored a candid misgiving towards the unpredictable trajectory of biotechnology. "It would take a brave man to predict where this is all going to come out."

The Delaware Biotechnology Institute has catalyzed a number of important academic-industrial partnerships. A notable example: a $250,000 allocation for renovating laboratories at Wesley College and Delaware State, enhancing research infrastructure. Another instance is the Integrated Network for Biomedical Research Excellence (INBRE) receiving a five-year, $17 million grant in 2004 to build state-of-the-art laboratories and fund 19 medical studies. This National Science Foundation endeavor led to the publication of approximately 100 medical journal papers. Additionally, Christiana Hospital and the University of Delaware collaborated for five years on *translational cancer research*, demonstrating a practical application of these partnerships in advancing medical knowledge and patient care in tandem. These alliances supported a spectrum of locally based bioscience companies, from start-ups to multinationals.

Continuing discourse around Delaware Biotechnology Institute mirrors a global conversation. The scientific community must balance both ethics and promise with precaution. Such discussions extend far beyond the small, yet ambitious, First State. *photo of David Weir and stromule: University of Delaware BioImaging Center*

Page 74 Delaware State University Icon

However, a growing restlessness steered him back toward academia. Wash initiated his graduate studies at Pennsylvania State, then transferred to Rutgers. There, in 1949, he acquired a master's degree in agriculture. That same year also marked the beginning of Ulysses Washington's distinguished time at Delaware State College, now Delaware State University. Dr. Howard Thomasson, then acting president, hired Washington to teach farm mechanics at a salary of $3,000. Before looking into Washington's remarkable tenure at Del State, one must understand the institution's historical underpinnings.

Delaware State College, established in Dover in 1890, is one of America's 19 public Black institutions known as the "1890 Land-Grant

Colleges." The foundation of DSU and its fellow institutions was structured from the start by the Second Morrill Act of 1890, which aimed to provide advanced educational opportunities amidst the era's racial discrimination. This context sets the stage for appreciating the enormous contributions Ulysses Washington would soon bring to DSU.

In 1949, the school had just gone through a growth spurt. The student body, 300 strong, was three times the 1942 enrollment. The campus library, a middling 6,000 books in 1942, by 1949 had expanded to 16,000. The USDA played a strong role in supporting and partnering with the agriculture department's programs starting around the time Washington joined the college. The new hire began as an assistant professor of agriculture education and farm mechanics. Land grant colleges emphasized practical training in the use of equipment and cultivation. Delaware State was expected to highlight such a curriculum and train students in fields where job opportunities were likely (i.e. preparing them for work in the dairy industry.)

Despite DSU's mandate via the Second Morrill Act to push agriculture, school enrollment tilted more toward teacher training. The agriculture department struggled during the 1950s, averaging only about 14 students enrolled a year. The real possibility loomed of the specialization having to be dropped. Ulysses Washington made possible the section's very viability throughout this lean period.

By the 1960s the mid-career scholar proved his adeptness in both academics and athletics by adding a coaching role with the Hornets football team. This opportunity allowed him to leverage his own undergraduate gridiron experience. Washington's coaching spanned 18 years, with a notable stint as head coach during 1965-66. He was especially proud to have coached John Land and Steve Davis, who went on to sign National Football League contracts.

Professor Washington was instrumental in the 1967 negotiation that allowed DSU to lease property to the Delaware Agricultural Museum, in return for an off-campus research farm near Kenton. Meanwhile, he stepped up to the position of Acting Chair of Delaware State's Department of Agriculture and Natural Resources. His appointment as Permanent Chair in 1971 marked a career milestone. Under the new chairman's leadership, the department boasted 12 research projects. These investigations soon encompassed all three Delaware counties. By Dr. Washington's retirement, department staff had expanded from five to thirty-five.

Eighty years after DSU was founded, the Association of 1890 Research Directors formed to boost research at Land Grant colleges. The nationally esteemed Professor Washington helped establish the association, advocating fervently for more funding. His efforts culminated in the U.S. Washington, Jr. Financial Anti-Discrimination Act. President Jimmy Carter signed the measure into law in 1978, improving research funding at 1890 Land Grants.

Delaware State's Board of Trustees in 1981 awarded Ulysses Washington an Honorary Doctor of Science. Widely esteemed as an educator and researcher, the new Dr. Washington went on to become a member of the Delaware Vocational Association, and the Board of Directors on both the Delaware Agricultural Museum and the Delaware Conservation Education Association.

As former chairman of Delaware State's Athletic Council, Washington proposed creating a Delaware Athletic Hall of Fame in 1985. "Ulysses aimed to elevate Delaware State athletics and honor its rich history," remarked George Robinson, then the athletic development officer. Delaware State had no formal system to acknowledge athletic excellence, despite a 70-year history of competition. A committee of former athletes and coaches affiliated with DSU convened to make the idea a reality. The first induction celebrated 98 notable individuals from different eras of Delaware State's athletic participation.

In 1993, DSU dedicated the Ulysses S. Washington, Jr. Cooperative Extension Center to honor the beloved educator. The acknowledgments continued with the naming of the Dr. Ulysses S. Washington Agricultural Extension Building in 1999 and the Science Laboratory in the University's Early College High School in 2018. Further honors include membership in the Delaware State University Alumni Hall of Fame; Pioneer Award as one of the first Extension administrators for 1890 Land Grant Universities; and induction into the George Washington Carver Public Service Hall of Fame in 2009.

From 1953 to 2004, the trailblazer marched as Grand Marshal at every Delaware State Convocation and Commencement ceremony—a 51-year stretch extending over a decade post retirement. From the late 60s until 2017, Dr. Washington resided on campus in a white house behind Loockerman Hall and adjacent to the college that he helped build. He credited Dr. Luna Mishoe, former DSU president, for granting him access to the residence for as long as he desired.

Ulysses S. Washington's larger-than-life persona continued to resonate right up until his passing on October 25, 2018. His exemplary leadership — evident in classrooms, on football fields, and through Congressional advocacy — has created a role model that endures. *Both photos Delaware State University/William C. Jason Library collection*

Page 75 University of Delaware Internet Research

David Farber's pupil David L. Mills, another trendsetter, addressed different yet equally integral challenges. Mills spearheaded Network Time Protocol (NTP) development starting in 1977. These efforts laid a cornerstone for modern data sharing infrastructures. Computers and networks before NTP operated on independent time systems. This lack of centralization could lead to a myriad of errors, particularly in fields where precise timing was paramount.

Mills introduced NTP as a network-wide solution for synchronizing computer clocks to a precise time source. "The strangest thing about the whole process is that we were inventing email, file transfer protocols and remote interactive access, using the very infrastructure that we were developing," Mills later marveled. NTP facilitated data's worldwide orderly flow.

David Sincoskie had a key role in the web's commercialization. He moved to New Jersey after the University of Delaware granted him a bachelor's degree, a master's degree, and a Ph.D. The electrical engineer began working for Bell Laboratories in 1980. His research gelled between 1986 and 1995, during which he ascended to a leadership position at Bell Labs' Bellcore. His guiding hand led the division to play a central role in transitioning telecommunications from circuit switching to packet switching. After his influential tenure there, Sincoskie joined Telcordia Technologies as the company's Senior Vice President of the Networking Systems Laboratory division. He pioneered the development of internet telephony in this new role.

The Institute of Electrical and Electronics Engineers recognized David Sincoskie's extensive contributions in 2003, awarding him the Fred W. Ellersick Prize for his development of broadband packet switching technologies over two decades. Sincoskie in 2008 returned to the University of Delaware. There, the renowned professor established the Center for Information and Communications Sciences to address national security.

Farber, Mills, and Sincoskie, all associated with the University of Delaware, uniquely contributed to the development and evolution of the online world. Their decades-long efforts vitally transitioned the internet from a concept to an indispensable tool. *Digital background courtesy Pixers.hk*

Made in the USA
Middletown, DE
04 October 2024

62018582R00075